Words of Praise for

Mending the Past and Healing the Future with Soul Retrieval

"Alberto Villoldo provides an awesome vision portraying the ancient shamanic worldview with that shown to be evident in quantum physics. Dr. Villoldo writes well, tells us an interesting story, and at the same time lets us see into the magical workings of the universe. But this is more than just a description—it is a path to well-being and self-healing, one you can take with the new universal soul realization offered by the author."

— **Fred Alan Wolf, Ph.D.,** the National Book Award–winning author of *The Yoga of Time Travel, The Eagle's Quest, The Spiritual Universe,* and many other books

"Alberto has that magical combination, fashioned by an open heart and a fine mind, of (1) the finest teachings of healers among primary peoples, (2) an understanding of modern science, and (3) an enchanting and practical way of sharing the wisdom with us through his words. Use this book to clear old traumas, and to awaken your own joy and gifts, both of which are precious to this world."

— **Brooke Medicine Eagle,** the author of *The Last Ghost Dance* and *Buffalo Woman Comes Singing*

"Alberto Villoldo is almost without peer in translating the understanding of ancient and tribal communities for the modern world. He is, moreover, an embodiment of these understandings."

— **Catherine Ingram,** the author of *Passionate Presence* and *In the Footsteps of Gandhi*

"This book is a wondrous journey filled with ancient wisdom particularly relevant to the predicaments of our modern life. Every reader will benefit from what Alberto Villoldo presents here; I highly recommend it."

— **Stephan Rechtschaffen, M.D.,** the cofounder and CEO of the Omega Institute

"Villoldo presents a vital way to retrieve your own soul so that you will thrive and not just survive. He guides us clearly and in a masterful way into our inner landscapes where healing and evolution occurs. This is important, and a much-needed work right now."

— **Sandra Ingerman,** the author of *Soul Retrieval* and *Medicine for the Earth*

MENDING
the PAST
and HEALING
the FUTURE with
SOUL
RETRIEVAL

Also by Alberto Villoldo, Ph.D.

Dance of the Four Winds (with Erik Jendresen)

The First Story Ever Told

The Four Insights

Healing States (with Stanley Krippner, Ph.D.)

Island of the Sun (with Erik Jendresen)

Millennium Glimpses into the 21st Century

The Realms of Healing (with Stanley Krippner, Ph.D.)

Shaman, Healer, Sage

Please visit Hay House USA: **www.hayhouse.com**
Hay House Australia: **www.hayhouse.com.au**
Hay House UK: **www.hayhouse.co.uk**
Hay House South Africa: **www.hayhouse.co.za**
Hay House India: **www.hayhouse.co.in**

MENDING
the PAST
and HEALING
the FUTURE with
SOUL
RETRIEVAL

Alberto Villoldo, Ph.D.

HAY HOUSE, INC.
Carlsbad, California • New York City
London • Sydney • Johannesburg
Vancouver • Hong Kong • New Delhi

Published and distributed in the United States by: Hay House, Inc.: www.hayhouse.com • *Published and distributed in Australia by:* Hay House Australia Pty. Ltd.: www.hayhouse. com.au • *Published and distributed in the United Kingdom by:* Hay House UK, Ltd.: www. hayhouse.co.uk • *Published and distributed in the Republic of South Africa by:* Hay House SA (Pty), Ltd.: www.hayhouse.co.za • *Distributed in Canada by:* Raincoast: www.raincoast. com • *Published in India by:* Hay House Publishers India: www.hayhouse.co.in

Editorial supervision: Jill Kramer • Editorial consultation: Nancy Peske, Chris Morris
Design: Tricia Breidenthal • Momentum tunnel illustration: Diana Hocking

Library of Congress Cataloging-in-Publication Data

Villoldo, Alberto.
Mending the past and healing the future with soul retrieval / Alberto Villoldo.
         p. cm.
ISBN-13: 978-1-4019-0625-2 (hardcover)
ISBN-10: 1-4019-0625-7 (hardcover)
ISBN-13: 978-1-4019-0626-9 (tradepaper)
ISBN-10: 1-4019-0626-5 (tradepaper)
1. Shamanism. 2. Soul--Miscellanea. 3. Mental healing. 4. Chakras. I. Title.
         BF1621.V55 2005
         131—dc22

2004028839

ISBN 13: 978-1-4019-0626-9
ISBN 10: 1-4019-0626-5

15 14 13 12   9 8 7 6
1st printing, May 2005
6th printing, December 2012

Printed in the United States of America

*To my mother, Elena Villoldo,
who showed me the way of love,
and to La Loba.*

Contents

Preface

This book is the result of more than 25 years of research and training with the shamans of the Americas. The rites of passage I underwent in the high mountains of the Andes and the low jungles of the Amazon adhered to ancient tradition and required months of preparation. My quest to discover the healing traditions of this continent was guided by an old Inka, don Antonio. My adventures with this renowned healer are chronicled in my earlier books *Shaman, Healer, Sage; Dance of the Four Winds;* and *Island of the Sun.*

The soul-retrieval techniques in this book represent my contemporary reinterpretation of ancient healing practices that are still in use in North and South America. Among Hispanic and Native American communities throughout the U.S., when children suffer from *susto* (or fright), they're taken to a special place to retrieve the part of their soul that was lost or taken from them; I've adapted and translated these practices within a modern scientific context.

Destiny-retrieval practices have been lost among most aboriginal societies. Yet I was very fortunate to spend many years with the *Laika,* master seers of the Inka nation, where I learned these skills. Please keep in mind that the practices I'm going to share with you in this book are extraordinarily powerful and effective, and must only be used with the strongest code of ethics and integrity. In fact, much of the shaman's lengthy training is spent developing a high sense of ethics founded on a deep reverence for all life. Only then can the techniques and processes be properly mastered and used to heal others. Similarly, a Western medical doctor spends at least five years learning his or her craft.

Is it prudent to turn my physical- or mental-health care over to someone who's taken a weekend workshop in shamanism or energy medicine? This is the quandary for Westerners who take a short course in the healing arts. If you have a calling to practice these healing arts, be sure to take the time to train with teachers whose integrity, wisdom, and technical knowledge will assist you in developing your individual spiritual gifts.

My own journey into shamanism was guided by my desire to become whole. In healing my own soul wounds, I learned to love myself and others. I walked the path of the wounded healer and learned to transform the grief, pain, anger, and shame that lived within me into sources of strength and compassion. At the Healing the Light Body School that I direct, every student embarks on a quest for self-healing in which he or she transforms soul wounds into sources of power and wisdom. Students learn that this is one of the greatest gifts that they'll later offer their clients: the opportunity to discover the power and wisdom within their own healing journey.

Of course, I'm not the first to bring to light the ancient healing practices of the Americas. The anthropologist Margaret Mead opened the door for all of us who follow in her footsteps; and my friend and colleague Sandra Ingerman, with her groundbreaking book *Soul Retrieval: Mending the Fragmented Self,* was the first to make us aware of the power and beauty of these ancient healing practices, as well as provide us with a practical guide for healing ourselves. A number of others, including Hank Wesselman and John Perkins, have also built bridges that have allowed many to cross into the realm of indigenous spirit.

Finally, I want to state that the healing methods in this book are *my own* synthesis and interpretation of ancient healing practices. I do not speak for my teachers, for the Inka, or for Native American shamans. Although I've had the privilege of training with the finest Inka medicine people, I make no claim to be representing a body of Inka traditions. The practices of soul retrieval and destiny retrieval described herein are adaptations of what I learned during my training as a shaman, and I take full responsibility for them.

— Alberto Villoldo, Ph.D.
www.thefourwinds.com

Introduction

During the 1980s, I spent countless hours in a laboratory studying the human mind, searching for some tangible evidence of the consciousness lurking within the gray matter inside our heads. I was fascinated by the mind's extraordinary power to create psychosomatic disease, and it was this fascination that led me into the field of psychology, and later, to medical anthropology.

After a while, I began to think that rather than hunting for scientific answers in millions of brain synapses, I might have to explore a different approach to investigating human consciousness. I began with the theory that in the same way that we can create psychosomatic *disease,* the mind must also be able to create psychosomatic *health.* I set out to look for experts who could provide me with insights into how we humans could train the mind to heal itself and to transform the body.

From my anthropological studies, I knew of indigenous cultures in South America where shamans were reported to perform miraculous healings, both in person and from a distance. I decided to travel into their worlds with a scientific mind, yet leaving myself open to what I might discover. I purchased a good hunting knife and a sturdy pair of hiking boots, and I set out from the confines of my laboratory at San Francisco State University on a quest that would take me to the jungles of the Amazon, and finally to Inka shamans living in remote villages thousands of feet up in the Andes mountains of Peru.

I was one of the first anthropologists to have extensive communication with these wisdom keepers, known as the *Laika.* Since they're among the last remaining Inka, they've had very little contact with outsiders, and their teachings have been undiluted by missionaries or other Western influences. More important to my studies, the Laika still practice healing techniques that their ancestors cultivated for thousands of years and handed down from teacher to student in their medicine societies.

At first, the shamans in each village I visited were very reluctant to share their heritage with me—a Westerner and a complete stranger—but I eventually gained their trust. On my early journeys, I observed that many children in the villages were suffering from the illnesses of civilization, including intestinal disorders that ran rampant among babies. Since the ailments didn't respond to local herbs and cures, I began to bring medications with me to treat the children. Over time, the villagers began to see me as a healer of sorts, so they introduced me to *their* healers, and through them I met many others.

Don Antonio Morales, who was on the faculty of the University of Cusco and was a full-blooded Inka, became my primary mentor. I walked with him through the high mountains of the Andes, meditating in sacred sites and ancient temples. I also studied with medicine women of the highlands who taught me about power animals and showed me how to merge my consciousness with that of a jungle cat and a condor. Despite my training in Western science, I learned to open my inner vision. I discovered the maps to the Lower World of our past and to the Upper World of our becoming, and the techniques of soul retrieval and destiny retrieval—the very same processes that you'll learn in this book.

The Different Worlds

The Laika divide the collective unconscious of all humanity into three parts: the *Lower, Middle,* and *Upper Worlds.* These aren't physical places, but rather archetypal and energetic domains. As June Singer, the renowned Jungian analyst, wrote: "The wonder of the collective unconscious is that it is all there, all the legend and history of the human race, with its unexorcised demons and its gentle saints, its mysteries and its wisdom, all with each one of us—a microcosm within the macrocosm. The exploration of this world is more challenging than the exploration of outer space."

The world we live in, where we work and raise our families, is the Middle World; the Upper World is the invisible domain of our destiny and our spirit; and the Lower World, where the record of all human history is held, is the realm of the soul. Now, in the Middle World, we perceive time to be linear—tomorrow always follows today—so it's difficult to imagine how we could travel into the past or future. But by using the technique of journeying that I'll detail, we can visit the Upper and Lower Worlds—and it's here that time loops and wormholes into the past and the future.

In this book, I'll teach you how to travel to the Upper World to find your highest destiny in order to manifest the meaning and purpose in your life. But you'll also journey to the Lower World, where your childhood and your former lifetimes reside, to recover the lost parts of your soul. These soul parts will take the form of beings: a frightened seven-year-old, an anguished mother, or even a cruel taskmaster. You'll learn their stories, heal their wounds, and write new contracts that will free them from their burdens; then you'll retrieve these healed soul parts and bring them back to the present. You'll discover your hidden gifts, which you may use in your everyday life in the Middle World, and you'll retrieve a power animal who will put you back in touch with your natural instincts.

The Four Chambers of the Lower World

The Lower World is the primordial Eden, which legend says we've all lost. It's an earthly paradise that you can return to anytime, where your lost soul parts have remained in grace and innocence. This realm is divided into four chambers, each containing a record of your soul's history.

1. The first of these is the **Chamber of Wounds,** where you discover the original wounding that caused part of your soul to flee and to derail the course of your destiny. Here you won't be looking for the most recent manifestation of this injury, which may be a lost relationship or a personal crisis, but for its *source.* It may be something that happened to you as a small child, or an incident that occurred while you were still in the womb. It's often a traumatic experience from a former lifetime.

Everyone has an original wound that replays itself in many guises. It becomes a recurring theme in life, oftentimes repeating a script of scarcity, loss, lack of love, betrayal, or abandonment within a family and across generations.

2. The second chamber is the **Chamber of Contracts,** where you'll discover the soul promises that you've made. Many of these will be terrible obligations that you agreed to before you were even born, and of which you have no conscious knowledge. Most were entered into during the fear and stress of your original wounding, and often you're unaware that they exist. In this chamber, you can renegotiate the terms of an agreement that was badly worded and that has sentenced you to a life of repeated suffering.

3. The third is the **Chamber of Grace.** Here you'll find your healed soul part, which is ready to return to you with all its life force. Grace is the fuel that propels you forward in life, what brings joy and peace. It isn't enough to journey to discover the pathology created by your wounds; you must also seek beauty, harmony, and the unique gifts of your soul.

Sometimes when I'm working with a client, I find that her life force has become like a small fire that's nearly disappeared from what was once a roaring, raging blaze. The flickering flame that's left is barely enough to warm the soul. (I see this often in my clients who are suffering from chronic fatigue, anxiety, and depression.) By retrieving her missing soul part, my client can then return to her natural state of grace and aliveness, and rekindle her passion for life.

4. The fourth chamber of the Lower World is the **Chamber of Treasures.** We tend to harvest those prizes that are closest to the surface, which suffice for an adequate and ordinary life. But we must dig deep in order to gather the most precious stones, silver, and gold buried far below. Like diamonds, the greatest treasures can only be extracted with significant effort. When I do a soul retrieval for a person who's having difficulty manifesting who he wants to become, I'll go into this chamber to help him retrieve an unexpressed creative or artistic gift. It's here, deep in the unconscious, that he can find the

resources that will help him live more fully. (I'll also retrieve a power animal that will help him recover his natural instinct.)

In each of these chambers, you'll read some of the books in the "library of your life" and uncover your deeply buried wounds, contracts, blessings, and gifts.

Journeying to the Past and the Future

I'm going to teach you how to retrieve your lost soul parts and recover the original clarity and brilliance of your soul. You'll navigate through the all-pervading matrix of light that organizes time into past, present, and future by *journeying*—a unique state of consciousness that you enter through guided meditations and breathing exercises. Journeying will allow you to revisit the past to heal events that occurred long ago and to find more desirable destinies for yourself and your loved ones.

Quantum physics has shown that the past and the future are connected in a noncausal but meaningful way. In the Amazon, I learned how to put these discoveries of physics to work in my own life. For example, my publisher assumed that the finished book you're reading is the result of my writing its 12 chapters. But I see the process differently: Before I started writing, I tracked forward along my destiny lines and found the one that contained the completed book. Because I was able to track into the future, I knew that my writing was being "pulled forward" and guided by the finished work. In other words, it actually wrote itself, since the manuscript was being guided by the already-published book. Journeying let me break free of living exclusively in linear time—it allowed me to track for a destiny greater than that scripted and defined by my history.

Destiny tracking is practiced by native cultures throughout the world, who perceive nature as a vibrant, pulsing field of energy. For example, the Aborigines of Australia understand the world as having been created by "song lines," or invisible trails representing the paths on which their ancestors walked and "sang" the world into existence.

In the Americas in the 1870s, the Osage, a Native American nation, tracked along similar destiny lines to learn where to relocate their tribe: Their chief selected a section of eastern Oklahoma for resettlement, doing so after tracking for the most desirable destiny for his people. Stories say that the land spoke to the people and told them that it would always take care of them. Indeed, the Osage became the richest people per capita in the world during the oil boom of the 1920s, thanks to an enormous supply of oil found on their lands. To this day, the Osage have contracts with some of the country's biggest oil producers.

In this book, you'll learn that after you mend the past, you can also heal the future by tracking for your highest destiny. Like the Osage, you'll find the places that are best for you to live, the work that's most meaningful for you, and the relationships that are the most fulfilling.

The Art of Healing

By practicing soul retrieval with hundreds of clients over the last 20 years, I came to realize that deep healing could occur in the space of days and weeks rather than months and years. This was the wisdom I'd been seeking—an understanding of the mind that goes beyond our physical bodies, in which the mind is the vehicle for awareness and the author of our health and our destiny. After two decades of research in the Amazon and the Andes, I've adapted ancient techniques into processes that we can use to mend our past and heal our destiny. These techniques interweave findings in anatomy, physiology, biology, and physics, and make these ancient healing practices eminently contemporary and scientific. Each year, hundreds of students at my teaching center, The Four Winds Society, learn how to employ these techniques to heal themselves and others.

But what does it mean to heal the future? *Healing,* you see, is different from *curing.* Although healing is very often accompanied by a cure, a cure alone seldom results in a healing. For instance, many of us know people who have undergone a coronary bypass or had a tumor removed, but who haven't healed their toxic relationships or changed their diet; consequently, their condition recurs months or years later. We also probably know individuals who have been in psychotherapy for years, yet they still can't find a healthy relationship or get over their anger at their parents. But then we may also know of those who say, "My cancer saved my life," because it gave them the opportunity to reinvent every aspect of themselves, from their diet to their relation-ships and careers.

In other words, curing is the business of medicine, and it involves eliminating symptoms; while healing is the crafting of a healthy lifestyle by eliminating the cause of suffering and disease and then creating a meaningful destiny. Ours is the practice of healing.

Western medicine cures the body, while psychology treats the mind—but healing attends to the soul and the spirit. The Laika believe that the physical world nests within the realm of the mind, which rests within the domain of the soul, which is held within the folds of the spirit. Spirit is the wellspring from which everything else emerges: It is pure light.

As seers who perceive the invisible world of energy and spirit, the Laika understand that *everything* in the universe is made of light, and that it forms and creates matter. In some things, light is bound very tightly, as in trees and stones, while in others it's more fluid, such as in rivers or in sunlight. Today, scientific discoveries confirm that when we look deeply into the heart of matter at the most fundamental level, all we find is vibration and light.

So, by working directly with the soul and the spirit, we can bring about change on all other levels, including the body and mind. Change on the level of the spirit transforms the world.

Using This Book

Please know that soul retrieval shouldn't be taken lightly. (In fact, I urge my students not to attempt to guide anyone else through a soul retrieval until they've mastered it themselves during their training.) The techniques in this book will help you with this process, but it may be very unsettling at the beginning, as you may have forgotten or repressed the deep wounds that caused your soul loss. However, through soul retrieval, you can finally reintegrate *all* aspects of your soul.

The processes in this book are immensely practical. In each chapter, you'll find guided meditations that will allow you to put journeying to work in your life right away. The more you practice these techniques, the greater your skill will become, and the more effectively you'll be able to heal yourself and track your destiny. I understand that it might be difficult to read the journeying exercises, some of which are quite lengthy, and then close your eyes and remember all the steps. I suggest that you read each exercise into a tape recorder so that you can play them back when you're ready to journey.

The first step you must take is to understand how time is experienced differently by the brain and the soul, and how our chakras (energy centers) are impacted by the wounds we've suffered, which I'll explain in the next chapter. Let's get started.

Part I

PREPARING YOURSELF for SOUL RETRIEVAL

CHAPTER ONE

The Physics of Destiny

I left my laboratory at the university to become lost in the Amazon. For three hundred million years, green life pollinated itself here into an infinite variety of vines, ferns, and twenty-story high trees. I gouged my leg on a fallen branch yesterday, and already there is green slime growing on the cut. I am becoming a walking biology experiment. Tomorrow, I arrive at the village where don Ignacio lives. He is a renowned healer, a hatun Laika, a master of the journey beyond death, a man who is both feared and loved in the region. People say that he can track your destiny the way another man can track a deer through the forest.

There is only one life form on the planet. And it has a sense of humor. DNA explores itself as frog, tapir, jaguar, human, orchid, bird, and even the pink-bellied dolphins that have made their way six thousand miles up the Amazon River to become freshwater fish. Had the shamans known about the double helix of life, they surely would have called it a god.

— from Alberto's journal

Many aboriginal cultures around the world share a belief that our bodies, as well as those of all living things, have energy centers known as *chakras*—spinning vortexes of light where energy is received, released, and exchanged with nature.

There are seven chakras that run along your spine. Shaped like fun-nels, the wide mouths extend one or two inches above the skin, and the narrow tips connect to your spinal cord. You receive impressions of your world through these energy centers: for example, you perceive love in your heart; sexuality, fear, and danger in your belly; and insight in your forehead. Through your chakras, you can cross over from the realm of matter of the body into that of light and spirit.

Your energy centers are surrounded by your luminous energy field or *aura* (which you'll learn more about in Chapter 12). In their healthy state, each energy center vibrates with one of the seven colors of the rainbow, giving your aura a glow and radiance.

Soul loss is recorded in your chakras: Each of them contains all the memories about the painful events that keep you bound to karma or fate. Different wounds affect different chakras, and when one is harmed, it loses vital resources. It leaks its essential fuel and becomes dull and grayish, so the emotions associated with this energy center also become muddled, and the radiance of your luminous energy field is dimmed.

In subsequent chapters, you'll learn how you can recover and reinstall these vital resources into the appropriate chakras during a soul-retrieval session. After journeying to discover the original wounding that caused soul loss, you'll be able to return the essence and energy of that soul part back to the wounded chakra.

The Chakras

Now let's become better acquainted with each energy center, beginning with the lower chakras. (I've described the chakra system in detail in my book *Shaman, Healer, Sage,* so I'll just provide a short summary of each here.)

The Lower Chakras

1. **The root chakra,** located at the base of the spine, is the gateway to Mother Earth and the feminine. When soul loss occurs in the first center, you can feel orphaned. You begin to distrust others and to look for security in material things. When you heal this center, all feelings of scarcity and lack disappear. (Many of your past-life stories are also contained in the first and second chakras.)

2. **The sacral chakra** can be found four fingers below the belly button. It activates the adrenal glands, and is home to passion, sexuality, and your early sense of self. This is where your fight-or-flight (stress) response resides, which triggers the production of adrenaline so that you can meet danger with heightened alertness and speed. When soul loss occurs at this chakra, the fight-or-flight response is turned on permanently.

My client Amy, for instance, had been experiencing the effects of heightened adrenaline for nearly five decades, ever since she'd been hit by a car while riding her bicycle as a child. Although she hadn't been injured in the accident, she remembered being thrown to the ground and how the car came to a sudden stop with her caught beneath it. Consequently, part of Amy had remained "trapped" under this automobile for years, afraid to venture out, powerless to fight *or* flee.

Through soul retrieval, Amy regained a lost soul part that showed her how to trust the world to be a safe place again. You see, when you heal the second chakra, you no longer live in fear, and the world ceases to be a menacing place.

3. **The solar-plexus chakra** influences how you express yourself in the world. When healthy, this energy center makes you stay true to your own nature. However, when soul loss occurs here, you're prone to feelings of sorrow and shame, or conversely, to ego inflation. You no longer know who you truly are. When you heal soul loss in this center, family and personal relationships become stable, and your sense of self becomes clear and defined.

4. The heart chakra, located at the center of the chest, is where you share and experience love. When soul loss occurs here, you confuse real love with infatuation; you can also become infatuated with the self. But when this center is healed, you're able to experience selfless love and forgiveness.

Since the heart is the axis of the entire chakra system, whenever I don't receive clear direction as to where a soul part needs to return, I bring it to my client's heart chakra. Its healing energy then gravitates to whichever chakra needs it most.

The Upper Chakras

While the lower chakras are of the earth, the upper chakras are of the sky, supported by the earth chakras much like high branches are supported by the trunk of a tree.

5. The throat chakra is located at the hollow of the throat and is your psychic center, giving you the ability to communicate without words. When soul loss occurs here, you're prone to sleep disorders, fear of speaking out or of being heard, weight-related disorders, and an inability to tell when people are insincere. If you have a wounded fifth chakra, you'll even have trouble being consistently truthful with yourself. When you heal this chakra, you can step into your personal power and rediscover your inner voice, and communicate clearly and truthfully.

6. The third-eye chakra is located in the middle of the forehead. Here you attain the knowledge that you and God are inseparable—through this chakra you're able to express the divine within yourself, and you're able to see it within others as well. When soul loss occurs at this center, you become overly cerebral and disconnected from your feelings. But when you heal it, you're able to experience spiritual truth and no longer feel separate from the divine.

7. The crown chakra is located at the very top of your head, and functions as a portal to the heavens in the same way that the root chakra functions as a portal to the earth. When soul loss occurs here, you feel a tremendous sense of isolation—but when it's healed, you're able to journey energetically through space and time, becoming one with heaven and Earth. (And it's only after we heal all of our own seven chakras that we can help another person to journey and recover a lost soul part.)

Two Additional Chakras

While in many Eastern traditions there's an assumption that all the chakras are contained within our bodies, the Laika believe that there are two additional ones that reach far beyond our physicality.

8. The **soul chakra** hovers above our heads like a radiant sun— we've seen this chakra illustrated as a golden halo over Christ and as a band of light surrounding Buddha. The soul extends luminous threads that connect us to rivers and forests, and to the place where we were born and where we now live. These threads also extend into our personal history and destiny. In later chapters, you'll learn to track along these energy strands, which I call *time lines,* to heal the past and influence the future.

The Laika discovered that this chakra is the grand architect of the physical body. When you die, the eighth chakra expands into a luminous globe that envelops the other chakras. After a period of atonement and purification between incarnations, it manufactures another body, as it has done over and over again throughout many lifetimes. The eighth chakra selected your biological parents, along with the home and circumstances you were born into.

Just as a carpenter builds a chair and later burns it in his fireplace, feeling no loss because he knows he can easily build another one, the eighth chakra feels no loss at the death of a body—it simply builds another one. If there happens to be a record of soul loss stored in this chakra, it's like a design flaw that's replicated with each new "chair" (or physical body). It will lead you to re-create families, life events, and relationships similar to those in your former lifetime in an attempt to heal this wound.

9. The **spirit chakra** resides outside the luminous energy field at the center of all creation and corresponds to that which is infinite. This is the matrix of the entire cosmos, the all-pervading luminous grid, transporting energy and information from one part of the universe to another. The Laika are able to sense and interact with this grid, and they use the practice of journeying to "dream the world into being," participating consciously in the evolution of life on Earth. Focusing our awareness on the ninth chakra allows us to journey into the past to heal bygone traumas, and into the future to retrieve our destiny.

Note that we cannot access the soul and spirit chakras until we heal the wounds and soul loss in chakras one through seven. Then we cease to identify with our past history and identify only with spirit.

The Timeless Now

*For us convinced physicists, the distinction between past, present,
and future is an illusion, although a persistent one.*
— Albert Einstein

For most of us, time is defined by ticking clocks, calendars, our past histories, and our future plans. You've probably been raised to believe that time "flies like an arrow"—that is, it irreversibly flows from the past to the present, like a leaf that falls into the water and then floats downstream. Psychologists look at childhood to find the cause of present suffering, and doctors look at personal and family medical histories for the origin of an illness or disease . . . all of which seems like common sense if you view your life as simply ruled by cause and effect. Science has named this *causality*, a "law" that says that the past always spills into and informs the present.

For the Laika, time zigzags between tomorrow and yesterday: It's like a river coursing lazily to the sea, and deep under its surface there's a tide streaming backward to its source and forward into infinity. While most people are content to float along the current, gifted individuals learn how to journey along these "time tides" to correct events that occurred in the past and to influence the future. That is, you can actually look into the future for the answer to a present question, and it will orchestrate synchronicity and serendipity to lead you to the solution. The future always spills into and can inform the present—if we invite it to.

You'll learn to use journeying to free yourself from linear time and cause and effect and to invite the future to lead you. While journeying, time ceases—there's only the "Timeless Now," the matrix of creation—and today no longer springs from yesterday. Journeying brings you outside of time's grip, to a state where everything happens concurrently.

Under the tutelage of the Laika, I learned how to use journeying to enter into the Timeless Now to heal the way in which events from my past lived within me. With training and practice, it will become just as easy for you to build your life from your destiny as it was in the way you're accustomed to—assembling your life from the broken fragments of the past brought forward to today. You can navigate into possible destinies and install a more desirable future into the present.

Journeying will allow you to break free of the cause and effect of karma. You can live your life with one foot in the domain of timeless spirit and one foot in the physical world. In doing so, you'll discover that both domains share common ground, and that the distinction between the past and the future truly is an illusion.

Un-spilling Milk

Your innate ability to experience time running simultaneously backward and forward is clouded by the fact that you haven't, for example, experienced a glass of milk "un-spilling" from the floor. The reason for this is the principle of *entropy,* which derives from the *second law of thermodynamics.* This principle states that disorder or chaos will always increase with time (you don't need to study at Harvard to understand this; you only need to have children). This movement toward chaos is evident all around us—our homes need repair, clocks wind down—so it's easy to go from the ordered state of milk in a glass to the disordered state of milk on the floor, from the past to the future, but not the other way around. The movement toward disorder seems inevitable, and the universe appears to be dying a slow, cold death.

However, living systems defy the second law: Life seeks order, beauty, and complexity, and it abhors chaos. Organelles come together to form cells, which team up to form tissues, which then join up to become organs that band together into humans, eagles, and all living beings. While nonliving things in the universe are breaking down, life continues building up into beautiful flowers, oaks, and whales.

In my years spent studying with the Laika, I've experienced how journeying allows us to access regions in the brain that can help us break free of the second law. Physics calls this process *nonlocality.*

Nonlocality

Quantum physics has shown that when you send two photons of light in opposite directions and you grab one with a polarizer, it affects the other instantaneously, suggesting that no time or distance intervenes between them. This is nonlocality, or the ability to influence events across a distance or through time.

Nonlocality has two characteristics: (1) There's no intervening energy or force needed to make it happen—it only requires intentionality, or the desire to make it so; and (2) there's no time or distance—that is, there's no message traveling from the present to the past, or into the future. The ability to influence events doesn't diminish over time or distance. In other words, there's no *now* versus *then;* instead, everything happens simultaneously.

The proof of nonlocality at the quantum level has been a recent scientific breakthrough, yet the Laika have long understood how distant events are linked. For most people, the closest experience they've had with this has come through prayer, which is something we're all familiar with (whether we actually practice it or not). At least 23 rigorous scientific studies have documented the power of prayer to heal individuals at a distance. Yet this is also true for studies conducted on plants: One found that mung beans sprout faster when they're prayed over. Now this cannot be explained by psychology or by the "placebo effect"—after all, you can't trick the mind of a bean into growing faster or resisting disease.

While we understand that prayer can influence distant events and bring about healing at a distance, what about our power to influence events that have already occurred? A study in the *British Journal of Medicine* discusses the results of an experiment in retroactive prayer. Researchers had a computer sort the ten-year-old hospital records of 5,000 patients with bloodstream infections into two random groups. One group was prayed over; one was not. The researchers then checked the records and found that those patients who had been prayed over had experienced shorter hospital stays and fevers, *even though the prayers took place ten years after the patients had been discharged.* The patients received the benefits of the prayers because of the nonlocal nature of time. The time of the prayer was actually concurrent with the time of the illness because in the Timeless Now, everything happens at once.

Nonlocality also explains that many events that we consider "psychic" are simply natural phenomena. For example, in the 1898 novel *Futility,* which was written 14 years before the *Titanic* set sail, a fictional ship named *Titan* was described in great detail. The similarities between the real and fictional ships were extraordinary: Each vessel had two masts and three propellers and was heralded as unsinkable—but most chillingly, each had a 3,000-passenger capacity and not enough lifeboats, and both experienced fatal collisions with icebergs in the month of April. Is this mere coincidence, or did the novel's writer track into the future and see the probable fate of the actual *Titanic?*

Experiments in quantum physics have demonstrated that the universe may be connected in a way that we can't perceive, at a level that includes our own consciousness and intentionality. We can rest assured that everything in the universe is interconnected in a luminous matrix that knows no distance, past, or future.

Journeying is an ancient technology that allows intentional interactions with an invisible energy that we're all part of. Through journeying I learned that I could shed my identification with my wounded self and with the painful events of my past. I discovered my destiny, which had always been available to me but not realized.

In the upcoming chapters, you'll learn the techniques to heal your past wounds and to change your destiny. You'll discover ancient maps for exploring the four chambers of the soul, and old myths describing the hero's journey will guide you. But first, we need to distinguish *destiny* from *fate* . . . which brings us to Chapter 2.

CHAPTER TWO

Transforming Fate into Destiny

I discovered that in the end, science is only a metaphor for nature, not nature itself. It's a metaphor that has replaced the old stories of the sky and earth gods. We no longer appease the lord of lightning or of wind—we can explain how low-pressure fronts cause tropical storms, but in the process we've lost the mystery and the wonderment at creation. We know why bees are attracted to flowers, but we forget to smell the roses or to be like the lilies of the field. . . .

I arrived at don Ignacio's this morning, following the trail, two feet wide. Here everything is overgrown, tangled, and wet. He lives in a village, or rather a large family compound at the edge of the Madre de Dios, the Mother of God River. I ask a boy and he tells me the village is called "El Infierno," or Hell. All around me are trees the size of office buildings. This is the land of giants. Parrots are hawking above, the river is flowing softly behind me . . . looks like paradise to me. Hell is where I come from, where concrete has overtaken nature.

El Infierno. "It's because of the birds," Ignacio would later tell me. "They squawk constantly, like missionaries."

— from Alberto's journal

Although the two terms are often used interchangeably, there's a marked difference between *fate* (which is known as *karma* among Eastern traditions) and *destiny* (also known as *dharma*). Fate is a course that's been predetermined by our family, our history, our genes, and our emotional wounds. We speak about the fate of nations with a sense of inevitability. We sometimes hear of two individuals meeting, or of a relationship breaking apart, and say that it was "fated to happen." And in many native cultures, there are two kinds of illnesses identified by healers: those that come from God, and those that come from man. Even though they may have identical symptoms, if an illness is seen as coming from God, there's nothing the healer can do other than alleviating the pain.

In other words, fate is the predetermined and seemingly inevitable series of events that happen to us. It seems unavoidable, and stalks us at every turn in our lives—for example, we leave one spouse, only to end up in the same relationship with another person. Fate is also deadly; in fact, it has the same origin as the word *fatality*.

Destiny, on the other hand, is the purpose and calling of a life, and it can be discovered and realized. Whereas the early Greeks believed that fate was spun from a certain thread, and that once it was woven into a cloth it was irreversible, they saw destiny as a force or agency that could intervene to reweave the cloth of fate. I believe that destiny can also happen without divine intervention—but it requires that you become conscious of your past wounds and respond to the calling you were born with, and you can then steer the course of your own life.

Destiny allows you to transcend fate and to live free of negative emotional and genetic programming. By stepping into your destiny, you can free yourself from an inheritance of breast cancer or heart disease, or from an emotional history that causes you to continually remarry an updated version of an unsuitable spouse. Destiny allows you to navigate life instead of stumble through it. When you step into your destiny, you can participate consciously in your own growth.

Biologists and the Laika have different understandings of evolution. Biologists think that it happens only *between* generations—that is, our children may be smarter and healthier than we are, but it's too late for the current generation to change. Science believes that our genes can't be altered, and we're all bound to inherit certain traits and tendencies from previous generations. So if a genetic predisposition runs in your family, your children's fate has been sealed: The breast cancer you inherited from your mother is just waiting to express itself, and the heart condition passed down from your father will spring up like a jack-in-the-box down the road. But the Laika understand that evolution happens *within* generations, so you can actually uncoil the layers of your genetic code to reinform your DNA and change your genetic fate.

I believe that we can change our destiny so that our children will inherit the healed traits we develop in our lifetime, as we uncoil the genetic code another strand. Through journeying, we can track a destiny in which we heal and age differently, one in which we avoid manifesting the ailments of our ancestors or reliving our childhood traumas. Journeying can guide us to grow new bodies informed not only by who we've been in the past, but by who we'll be 10,000 years from now.

The Quest of Parsifal

The 12th-century myth of Parsifal and his quest for the Holy Grail illustrates how we can search for and discover our own grails, thus transforming fate into destiny. Since this legend has been one of the most enduring and influential in our history, I've chosen to use it to help us understand the quest for destiny.

When the tale begins, Parsifal is a sheltered young boy. His mother, Heart's Sorrow, has already lost her husband and two sons in battle. Fearful that Parsifal will want to follow in their footsteps and become a knight and die an equally horrible death, she raises him in the forest far from civilization. Heart's Sorrow lives to protect her son from life.

One morning when Parsifal is playing in the woods, he comes upon a group of five knights dressed in shining armor and carrying long lances—and he's irresistibly drawn to their world of adventure. He's so taken by the gallant knights and their finery that he immediately decides to leave home and become a knight himself. His terrified mother pleads with him not to leave her, but Parsifal is determined to travel to the court of King Arthur and join his legendary Round Table. The young man receives his mother's tearful blessing, along with a simple homespun garment to wear. She tells him that he must respect all women, and he shouldn't be curious or ask any questions. With these gifts and warnings, Parsifal sets forth upon his quest to become a knight and to fulfill his fate.

When the boy arrives at King Arthur's court dressed in his mother's homespun garment, he asks to be knighted, and the country lad is laughed out of the hall. But Parsifal insists again and again, until he's finally granted an audience with the king. Among the members of the court is a lovely maiden who hasn't laughed or smiled in six years. Legend has it that she'll only laugh again when the finest knight in the world appears. Upon seeing Parsifal, she bursts into delighted laughter, startling the court. Who is this boy who's done what no other could? Can the foolish and untested Parsifal truly be the knight for whom they've been waiting?

The king tells Parsifal that to join the Round Table he must battle and defeat the Red Knight, the most fearsome warrior in the kingdom. He also tells the lad that he can have the Red Knight's horse and armor if he wins them from him in battle. Parsifal challenges the dreaded knight and, despite his inexperience, kills him with a stroke of luck. Victorious, Parsifal puts the Red Knight's armor over his homespun garment—and Arthur grants him his knighthood.

Parsifal's next task is to find the Holy Grail and return it to King Arthur's court. A wise old man, Gournamond, provides him with valuable instruction to guide him in his quest. Gournamond is stern in his advice: If Parsifal should ever find himself within the Grail Castle and come upon the holy relic, he must ask the question, "Whom does the Grail serve?"

Before embarking upon his knightly adventures, Parsifal decides to visit his mother to show her his accomplishments—but when he arrives at her door, he learns that she died of grief upon his departure. Torn apart by guilt, Parsifal continues on his way and soon finds Blanche Fleur (White Flower), a beautiful damsel whose castle is under siege.

She implores Parsifal to save her, and he charges into battle, valiantly defeating her attackers and winning back her kingdom. After the battle, he spends a single chaste night with Blanche Fleur, and in the morning, he continues on his hunt for the Holy Grail.

One day while seeking lodging for the evening, Parsifal comes upon some peasants who tell him that there's no shelter for 30 miles. But soon he finds a man fishing alone in a boat on a lake. The fisherman invites Parsifal to stay at his home nearby, gives him directions, and sends him on his way. To the young knight's surprise, the fisherman's home is actually the legendary Grail Castle. When Parsifal crosses the moat, he finds himself in a sumptuous, dreamlike setting, with a court of 400 knights and ladies surrounding the Fisher King, who lies in pain upon his litter, suffering from an unhealed wound to his thigh that was incurred much earlier. Parsifal realizes that the man he mistook for a simple fisherman was actually the Fisher King.

A great banquet is under way, during which the Fisher King gives Parsifal a sword. As part of the festivities, the Holy Grail is brought out and passed around the court. Everyone drinks from it and is granted a wish, except for Parsifal and the Fisher King, who can't drink from the Grail until his wound is healed. All through dinner, Parsifal sits silently, heeding his mother's warning not to ask any questions. The entire court observes him keenly, since they've been waiting a long time to see their prophecy fulfilled—legend has it that one day a naïve youth will appear at the castle and ask the "Grail question," thereby finally releasing its power and healing their king.

But Parsifal never speaks, and the next morning he finds the castle empty. He continues on, his new sword strapped to his side, as the Grail Castle vanishes behind him. Over the years, he pursues a long series of knightly accomplishments—slaying dragons, conquering enemy knights, rescuing fair maidens, and fulfilling the greatness that King Arthur saw in him. Parsifal's reputation for knightly prowess spreads, and word gets back to King Arthur, who asks to have the knight brought back to his court. A great festival and tournament are held in Parsifal's honor, and he's accorded the highest prestige and respect of any knight. However, at the height of the celebration, a hag appears. In front of everyone, she recites a litany of Parsifal's many sins, faults, and misdeeds, the most egregious of which is his failure to ask the Grail question when he had his opportunity.

Humiliated and humbled by the hag, Parsifal sets off once again in search of the Grail Castle, but all he finds are more battles and more hardship. One day in the autumn of his life, he finally comes upon a group of pilgrims who berate him for wearing his battle armor on Good Friday, one of the holiest days of the year. They lead him to an old hermit living deep in the forest who, just like the hag, chastises the knight for his failure to ask the Grail question.

When Parsifal strips himself of his armor and removes the home-spun garment that he's worn for so many years, the old hermit finally directs him to the Grail Castle. Now, at the end of his years of adventure, he's finally given another opportunity to prove himself in the most important of his tasks.

Parsifal finds the castle, and he steps forth and asks the magic question ("Whom does the Grail serve?"). At long last, all rejoice. The Holy Grail is passed around, the Fisher King is able to drink from the cup, and he's finally healed.

What We Learn from Parsifal

This myth tells us what's required in order to change our life from one in which we're controlled by fate to one in which we actually fulfill our destiny. When the story begins, Heart's Sorrow tearfully sends her son on his way in the garment she's made, admonishing him to ask no questions and to respect fair maidens. She then dies, enacting the worst nightmare of any responsible "good boy"—that if he leaves his mother and becomes independent, she'll die without him.

The homespun garment represents the curse of Parsifal's ancestors, the original mother wound, which prevents him from maturing. As long as he wears this garment, the relationship between him and his mother is frozen in an immature, dependent state. And because his mother has begged him not to, the boy fails to ask the Grail question. In doing so, he misses a crucial window of opportunity, given to him in his youth, to step into his destiny. It will take him an entire lifetime to find such a window again. Likewise, many of us are given a taste of the Grail early in life—golden opportunities that present themselves in the form of the right person to marry or the right career choice, for example—but we fail to take action. And then many years go by until we make our way back to our destiny and our true calling.

In many cultures around the world, such as the Hopi, the Celtic, and the Yoruba of sub-Saharan Africa, when a boy reaches adolescence, he's taught to embrace the earth as his eternal mother and to regard the heavens as his steadfast father. He learns that his place is out in the world—his biological mother and father can no longer provide what he needs. This no longer happens in Western cultures, where we seek to shield our children from the world. Cultural rites of passage, such as bar mitzvahs, confirmations, and 18th-birthday celebrations are meant to usher our children into maturity and independence . . . yet they've been deprived of meaning and instead have become parties for the sake of festivities and gift-giving.

Many of us never cut the apron strings of childhood, so we spend too many years blaming our mothers for our problems or running home to our parents for them to fix things. Like Parsifal, we're held back by constricting parental ties that stifle us from healing our own wounds—and, just like him, we need to remove our homespun clothes to find our own place in the world.

The Hag and the Daimon

Lots of people conspire to keep us bound to our fate. When Parsifal finds Blanche Fleur, for example—whose very name is the ultimate symbol of purity—she becomes his lifelong inspiration, driving him to protect what's pure and to fight for good over evil. Following his mother's advice, Parsifal never consummates his love for Blanche Fleur, and he refuses to allow himself to seduce her or to be seduced by her. Their single night together is devoid of intimacy, and there never is a second night.

Obviously, if Blanche Fleur were a real woman, this "relationship" would be an absurd cartoon, idealized to the point of misery. Can you imagine spending your entire life seeking a woman of absolute purity? Longing for a woman with whom you'd spent a single night? Certainly no flesh-and-blood female could ever compare to this idealized vision!

This is why it's important to understand Blanche Fleur as what Carl Jung called the "anima," or inner feminine. *Anima* is the Latin word for "soul." When you recover the wholeness of your soul and follow "her" guidance, you can break free from the curse of your ancestors and their lives of suffering and illness.

The Greeks called this aspect of the soul one's *daimon,* or our genie or guardian angel. The daimon will guide us throughout our life as long as we respect and stay true to her. If a man stays true to his inner guidance, for instance, he'll grow and mature as a result—but if he tries to avoid his inner feminine, he'll instead try to find her in physical form and marry his idealized image of the feminine instead of a real woman. He might run from woman to woman, subconsciously seeking out his inner feminine in corporeal form and insisting that his partner fit his illusion of how a woman should look and be. Likewise, if a woman is seduced by the myth of material beauty, then she'll never be able to find the beauty of the feminine within.

The myth of Parsifal reminds us that it isn't always easy for us to stay true to our own daimon. This is why the hag appears at the court: to expose the flawed man beneath the armor. The hag or crone (from the Greek *chronos,* which means "time") is the daimon reappearing and demanding attention. This figure appears in many myths, folktales, and legends as a speaker of the truth, usually telling the hero the things he doesn't want to hear, showing his neglected soul parts. In our own lives, the hag comes to us as an unpleasant "reality check," or a defining life experience such as the severing of an important relationship; being fired from a job; enduring an illness, a crisis, or a divorce; or losing something that we've held central to our being.

In the Parsifal myth, the hag's purpose is to show our hero that despite the fact that he has the right knightly persona, what's inside is unhealthy—he's lost his soul. He's been single-minded in the pursuit of his external self at the expense of his daimon. By the end of the story, his suit of armor has become a prison of material achievements, and he is lost within it. He has no love or human comfort, and he's failed in the one quest that has any meaning: finding the Grail.

When the hag humbles Parsifal, exposing all his dark aspects and none of his glory, he's devastated. Everything he values has been shown to be a farce. It's in this devastation that he's forced to reevaluate his life's purpose, to ask the question: "What is the meaning of my life?" This is Parsifal's turning point, the crucial moment in which he's finally compelled to get back on track with his life's quest.

Yet despite this experience, Parsifal only knows how to keep doing what he's always done. He returns to his horse and armor, but now his knightly achievements have no significance for him. He knows that despite his desire for something more meaningful, he's caught in the wheels of fate, living out a role handed down to him by his father and clothed in the garment woven by his mother.

The hag is the sacred feminine, the soul, making its appearance as the wise old woman. After suffering from years of neglect, she resurfaces to awaken Parsifal to the fact that he's going through the motions of life without joy and with no idea how to fix it. This is how the pious pilgrims find him when they ask him why he's dressed for war on one of the holiest days of the Christian calendar. They lead him deep into the forest, another symbol of the dark feminine. The old hermit sets him on the path that will lead him to the Grail Castle, where he's at last able to find his voice and ask, "Whom does the Grail serve?"

Parsifal is finally allowed to escape his fate of living and dying by the sword, as his father and brothers did before him, and he can now live a life of the spirit. The Grail Castle is a metaphor for coming into his destiny, which was always there for Parsifal; he just needed to be ready for it. When he finally looks within himself, he finds that the Grail Castle and the Holy Grail are just around the corner for him to embrace.

One of the lessons we learn from this story is that while our fate might seem inescapable, the Grail Castle (our destiny) is always waiting around the bend. Certainly, there are times in all of our lives when we find ourselves asking, "What is my life's purpose?" And while the story of Parsifal is traditionally used to illuminate the life quest of men, women face this same dilemma: "When will I be done with the battles?" they ask. "When will I be able to put my sword down?"

The myth of Parsifal suggests that after blundering our way along much of our life's path, for true fulfillment we must finally come to a place where we turn things over to a power larger than ourselves—be it God, our life's calling, or another form of the Grail. In the following chapters, we'll embark on this quest by employing the faculties of the "god-brain."

The Four Regions of the Brain

The reason that Arthurian legends have become so etched into our collective imagination is because they depict the actual life's journey that each of us must travel to discover our destiny. Likewise, we can make the journey toward our destiny over the course of many years (or many lifetimes), or we can travel through sacred territories and mythical landscapes in a much shorter time by using the process of journeying.

For the Laika, journeying isn't an exercise in the imagination—it's very real. This is difficult for those of us in the West to understand because we're so driven by precepts and rules. We distinguish between what obeys a set of predictable rules (such as the laws of physics), and what's imaginal. The Laika believe that *everything* is imaginal. Whatever we perceive is a projection of our inner world, and the world perfectly mirrors the condition of our soul. What we think of as the world of our imagination, the seers of old consider as real and tangible as our very physical world.

To access the imaginal world, we need to enter into special states of consciousness that are very different from our ordinary daily consciousness. These are the states that have been cultivated by mystics, monks, saints, and yogis; it's the "quiet mind" of the Laika and the Buddhas. This heightened awareness gives us access to our god-brain.

Although our brain doesn't create consciousness—it's far more likely that consciousness created the brain as a means to perceive itself—there are regions in the brain that become active when we enter certain states of awareness. For example, when we're angry, there's a region in the brain that lights up, while another region only becomes active when we're joyful, in love, or in meditative bliss. This is because the human brain is divided into four "sub-brains" that developed at different evolutionary stages. Each governs a different aspect of human nature:

1. The primitive, **reptilian brain** is charged with the biological functions of the body, such as controlling breathing, body temperature, and other autonomic systems. For this brain, destiny equals the preservation and continuation of life, and it measures time as the interval between meals and sex. This region evolved millions of years ago, and it contains the medulla and cerebellum.

2. The more complex and emotional **limbic brain** is in charge of family and culture. Anatomically, it enfolds the reptilian brain like a baseball glove. It holds the fabric of society together by subsuming the good of the individual for that of the tribe. Religion and law are both products of our limbic brain; in fact, five of the Ten Commandments—the prohibitions against murder, theft, adultery, lying, and envy—are designed to control the impulses of this region. I like to refer to this as our "monkey brain" because of its instinctual programs that are referred to lightly as the "Four F's"—fear, feeding, fighting, and fornicating.

If we're traumatized or wounded during childhood, the programs of the monkey brain will make us hoard material things, see strangers as enemies, build weapons of mass destruction, eat and drink excessively, take sexual partners indiscriminately, and live in fear of the unknown. This is the brain of superstition and most primitive religions, and it experiences time as moments of safety, fear, or lust. The limbic brain is in the driver's seat when fate is operating—here, destiny is subdued by an unstoppable desire for safety. Over millennia, shamans have discovered that techniques employed in journeying (which we'll explore in later chapters) override the four primary programs of the limbic brain, so we can live free of fear, anger, scarcity, and lust.

3. The **neocortex**, or "new" brain, first appeared 100,000 years ago in an evolutionary quantum leap in which the human brain doubled in size over approximately ten generations. The neocortex is

shared by all higher mammals and is our "scientist brain." Since it's the brain that invented timepieces, it lives by the clock.

The neocortex is also the fiercely individualistic brain of entrepreneurs and explorers. It gave rise to the Industrial Revolution and the space race, and the Constitution and the Bill of Rights. For this brain, destiny is about becoming an individual distinct from the masses. Many societies ruled by warlords and tribal chieftains find our desire for democracy utterly incomprehensible because they're still dominated by the limbic brain, which values the law of the pack over the freedom of the individual.

4. Finally, the **prefrontal cortex**, or **god-brain**, is a structure we share in its full expression with whales and dolphins, even though the hardware is present in all the higher mammals. It's located in our foreheads above our eyebrows—in fact, Neanderthals were known as "low brows" because they lacked this brain unit.

Imaging studies show that the prefrontal cortex is active during mystical and spiritual experiences. Buddhist monks who enter into the state of *samadhi* (or the experience of oneness with all life) display neural activity almost exclusively in this region of the brain; meditation has also been found to trigger dramatic changes in this region's electrical activity. The god-brain transcends individuality, seeking oneness with everything, and it regulates the aggressive and fearful impulses of the monkey brain. For the god-brain, time is fluid, running backward and forward as in dreams.

Awakenings

The monkey brain brings you to your first awakening, which occurs when you realize your own mortality (usually in your 30s or 40s). Animals are aware of death, but apparently don't realize that they're going to die. Similarly, children know that death happens to a pet, a friend, or a relative, but they don't understand that it will happen to them or that it's permanent. The monkey brain lives in fear of death.

The second great awakening occurs when you realize your trans-temporal nature—the undying, infinite self—which the god-brain can bring about. The god-brain understands that consciousness cannot die, and it allows us to live free from fear. Brilliant scientists, artists, shamans, and mystics have accessed its capabilities to produce their finest work. After returning from one such trance journey, the poet Samuel Taylor Coleridge jotted down the finished version of the poem "Kubla Khan." Mozart was reputed to have been able to hear an entire symphony playing inside his head, and he had to work furiously to transcribe the notes as fast as he heard them. This is the same brain that brings Parsifal to the Grail Castle and lets him discover whom the Grail serves.

Parsifal's Journey and Our Own

The myth of Parsifal teaches us that we can only heal ourselves by serving the sacred. This is the job of the god-brain, which goes beyond selfish, personal desires. When Parsifal asks the Grail a question and thus puts himself in service of it, the Fisher King and the knights and ladies of the court are healed. Through his lifelong pursuit, Parsifal teaches us that even though we may urgently wish to step beyond fate, we don't always know how to find the path to destiny.

Like Parsifal's quest, your journey to destiny will have many passages, not all of which will be comfortable or easy. You'll be led down dark corridors that force you to look into the eyes of the hag and reintegrate the unhealed parts of yourself. You'll explore your past, from former lifetimes to early childhood. You'll retrieve your lost feminine (your daimon) by healing your splintered soul parts, and explore the contracts which keep you bound to your ancestry or genes, just as Parsifal was bound to his mother by his homespun garment. You'll also learn how to recover the grace that will allow you to experience your life to the fullest. This is no different from Parsifal's learning to find his voice so that he could ask the magic question, which opened the gateway to his destiny.

In later chapters, you'll learn how to access the unique states of consciousness of the god-brain. The method we're going to learn—journeying—has been practiced by the Laika for millennia. These advanced healers follow "the pathless path"; likewise, you'll journey along your own unique path to move beyond the confines of your fate. We'll exchange the language of the neuroscientist for that of the Laika as you learn to journey into the Lower World (the past) and then to the Upper World (the future). But now, let's become more familiar with the place we'll be journeying to.

CHAPTER THREE

Mapping the Soul

The old man had been preparing his mind-altering brew since sunrise. An hour after the sun had set over the canopy of the rain forest, we each held a glass full of the bitter drink. It was made from ayahuasca, the legendary vine of death.

The Amazon Laika believe that to journey into the Upper and Lower Worlds (what we Westerners would call the "unconscious" and "super-conscious"), one has to step outside of time. The vine of death helps you do this, showing you every part of yourself that has died, as the hag does. The ruthless crone shows you everything that you've kept hidden inside—every fear, every judgment. And then the shaman wrenches it out of you and pulls it up from its roots, which are tangled in your every cell . . . they call it "exorcising death." The lore in this part of the rain forest is that once you've exorcised the death that lives within you, you can never again be claimed by it, because you've been claimed by <u>life</u>. Death stalks its prey within time—it waits for us at the end of every minute, every second. You step outside of time, and you become invisible to death.

The jungle pulsates in the night. The steady, sweltering hiss of the day gives way to the chant of a million insects. Somewhere a deep resonant hum was matching this tempo, and I looked out to see the old man silhouetted against the path of moonlight on the lagoon. The murmur of his chant was

*synchronized to the cadence of the jungle. I could not make out
the words of his song, but the verse changed four times as he
turned and faced each of the four directions.*
"Tonight we will bring the death out of you," he told me.
— from Alberto's journal

For years, psychology searched for the soul, first in the heart, and eventually in the brain. Finding no evidence for its existence, psychology gave up, leaving exploration of the soul to artists and poets.

Soul is the best word we have for that essential part of ourselves that seems to have preceded our entry into this world, yet also endures beyond our lifetime. For the Laika, the eighth chakra is the soul, which retains the memories of all the many incarnations we've had prior to this one and also contains the potential for who we can become.

Medicine people refer to this part of us as a seed that can grow and manifest if properly cultivated. Just as the acorn has the memory of the mighty oak living within it, it also needs to germinate in order to grow into a tree. Without the maturation process, the acorn remains a hard nut of unused potential; likewise, if a seed is left untended, it can wither or fail to reach its fullest expression.

The soul's journey is one of developing the great promise that each one of us carries within. As my mentor once told me, "We're here not only to grow corn, but to grow gods." In this book, we'll use the process of journeying to germinate our seeds so that they can take root and thrive, and to allow our divine nature to blossom. When a seed is neglected, it will produce a bitter fruit, but when it is tended to, it will provide a sweet bounty for ourselves and others. Only the seeds that we nurture will bear fruit.

There's an old Cherokee tale in which a man tells his grandson, "There are two wolves fighting within me. One of them is angry and hateful, the other is generous and compassionate." When the boy asks, "Which one will win, Grandpa?" the old man answers, "The one I feed."

The Source of All Life

What we refer to in psychology as the *subconscious,* the Laika represent as the Lower World—the rich, moist, feminine earth where the seed of our potential begins the journey to conscious awareness.

In mythology, the feminine often has three faces—virgin, mother, and crone—which are actually all aspects of a single archetype, the Great Mother. She resides, metaphorically, in the life-giving world deep within the earth—in fact, she's the very personification of the earth. It's what the Inka refer to as the *Pachamama,* the mother from whom we originally came, and to whom we eventually return. Even in Western mythology, we learn that we come from the dust of the earth, and that "to dust we shall return."

Native American cultures believe that all life sprouts forth from the hidden, Lower World. When a part of the soul fragments, it returns to the dark, feminine womb of Mother Earth, leaving behind a void that we try to fill with anything that will stop the hurt. As in our metaphor of the soil nourishing the seed, the Lower World is a living, life-giving place to which we can journey for restoration and rejuvenation.

This isn't true for us Westerners, though: Judeo-Christian tradition and Greek and Roman mythology see the Lower World as a place where we bury our dead. We associate the deep earth with hell and fire and brimstone—we believe it to be a place of torment and suffering. We don't see the earth as the origin of our life; instead, we look to images of our ancestors or photographs of our biological relatives as the place from which we come. In the West, we aren't children of the earth—we're children of humans.

Because of the Native Americans' deep appreciation for Mother Nature, it was befuddling when missionaries first told them that "heaven is up and hell is down." It was incomprehensible to them that Mother Earth, the source of all life, could be a baneful, horrible place where spirits suffer and pay for their sins in eternal damnation. To the indigenous Americans, the earth was a fertile place of renewal, a rich terrain into which they could journey to retrieve parts of a person's original "seed" that had splintered off as a result of trauma or pain.

The Lower World is a place where we can find the seven-year-old who fled because she couldn't stand the pain being inflicted on her by bullies, or the "seed potential" that was lost in a previous lifetime when someone was burned at the stake. The Lower World, the belly of the Great Mother, is the domain that protects our fragmented soul parts until they're ready to be brought back safely into the Middle World of our everyday consciousness.

The darkness that's represented by the Lower World is where we hide the things we no longer want to see. For example, I frequently run into instances of child abuse among my clients. In psychology, we look at how this experience may have been repressed and how it lies buried in our unconscious; then, through psychotherapy, we attempt to unearth and understand it. Yet Carl Jung himself observed how limited our understanding of the psyche is when he said, "Our personal psychology [and] the archetypes are the great decisive forces. They bring about the real events, not our personal reasoning and practical intellect. . . . The archetypal images decide the fate of man."

When a child is abused or traumatized, a fragment of his soul breaks off and returns to the archetypal domain of the Great Mother for the protection that his biological mother could not provide. This soul part is actually a portion of life energy that's now unavailable for his growth.

When I meet such a person, I recognize that areas of his development may have been arrested at a very young age. For example, a 40-year-old will have an argument with his spouse and revert to the behaviors and feelings of a 12-year-old. Inevitably, the original soul wound occurred at that earlier age, stunting this person's growth. I'll retrieve this lost soul part and reintroduce him to an aspect of himself that will allow him to begin to heal and thrive. This requires that my client remember an event from him past—often one that he has forgotten. When he "sees" this incident, which may be the way he died or suffered in a previous lifetime or a trauma from this incarnation, tremendous healing begins.

Dr. Brian Weiss, a past-life researcher and author, has documented hundreds of cases in which his patients were relieved of physical and emotional symptoms when they observed incidents from an earlier lifetime during past-life regression. I've learned that while observing these painful events is immensely transforming, it's only the first part of the process—you must also coax the soul part to return, then tear up or rewrite archaic soul contracts that have ceased to serve you, and finally track a future destiny that you can install into the present.

Although I'm trained both in psychology and the traditions of the Laika, I've found that one soul-retrieval session can accomplish what may take many years to heal employing psychotherapy. This is because to recover our innocence and trust in life we must renegotiate obsolete soul contracts and discarding limiting beliefs, which happens during the soul-retrieval journey. In addition, the language of the soul is very different from what we use in therapy and counseling. It's rich in image, myth, archetypes, and mystery—full of poetry and magic, it speaks to intuition and love. *Abandonment, fear, insecurity,* and *childhood trauma*—all of these terms belong to the intellect. I'm convinced that when we only have these words to explain our childhoods, it's a sure sign that we're suffering from soul loss, because the soul's very words have vanished.

At The Four Winds Society, my students are professionally trained to perform soul retrievals for other people, which is a delicate art. For example, my student Claire was able to use journeying to help her family heal at the end of the life of her mother, Anne. Anne had entered the hospital with a blood clot (a complication of her chemotherapy treatments) and she'd gone into kidney failure and toxic shock. Here's Claire's story:

> My mom was uncomfortable and emotionally detached from all of her children, even the grandkids. She was irritable, sick, and tired, and had no desire for visitors. I knew that her condition was critical and that she had a lot of fear concerning death. When I journeyed, my hope was to find the missing piece of her soul, which would then give her the hope to live and fight for her health. In my journey I met a beautiful being of white light—my heart was filled with its love and beauty. I brought this being back and blew it into my mother's heart chakra (she was still asleep).

About 15 minutes later, Mom opened her eyes with a start and looked out at me with such love that I got tears in my eyes, and my heart felt like it stopped for a moment. She was glowing! The energy shining from her entire being was breathtaking. My brother dropped the phone he was on and stated that she looked beautiful. Seconds passed as we looked on in amazement. Then, gently, she closed her eyes and fell back asleep. I felt like I'd done exactly what I needed to do, whatever the outcome of her health.

Later the doctor came in to tell us that there was nothing more they could do, so Mom was taken off the kidney support. I was quite calm as the doctor told me this, and I thanked him for all he'd done to try to help my mother.

Each of Mom's children, grandchildren, nieces, nephews, and siblings came to see her. She'd wake up when one would enter the room, shoot them a look of love, and tell them how much she loved them and how wonderful they were, and then she'd drift back to sleep. Everyone left the room deeply moved by the expression of her love. The kids were the most touching of all as they said, "She held my hand, she told me she loved me, she told me how special I was."

Mom had never been very expressive, so the fact that she was able to reach out to each person in this way surprised everyone. She never acknowledged her imminent death, but there was no fear, only love. She passed away peacefully that evening.

This soul journey brought back a lost part of my mother's soul that, once reintegrated into the whole, allowed her to break with the past and finally express love.

We all have soul parts that have splintered off. Once we recover them, dramatic changes occur in our lives.

Fishing in the Deepest Waters

Buried in the vast unconscious domain of the Lower World is the anima—the trusting, loving, innocent, feminine aspect of ourselves. This is the part of ourselves that we've abandoned or was taken from us by the great flood of childhood conflict or past-life trauma. In order to remain whole, it fled—leaving just the wounded self behind.

In order to heal the soul and find that missing part, we must go fishing in the deepest waters of the psyche, where we haven't gone before. This sort of healing can't happen when we're angling from the shore, where we rework everyday concerns. No, when we meet the soul in its own domain, the tools of psychology fall short. Psychology is like the fisherman who baits his hook, drops his line over the side, and brings whatever bites up on the deck of consciousness. We need to learn to jump over the side and follow the currents into the Lower World to explore its mysteries before we can really bring our catch to the surface. And what we find in those deep waters may unsettle and even frighten us.

We may think that we want to confront these lost parts of our soul, but when we finally do, our fears will often make us want to bludgeon them—after all, they can be scary and repulsive. In psychology, we're taught to analyze these aspects of ourselves, but in soul retrieval, we neither dissect nor deny these lost soul parts—instead, we acknowledge and heal them, and integrate them back into the whole of our being.

Of course, this is not an easy process. Setting your life in order again is often a cataclysmic event, since your world has been turned upside down. It can be tempting to tell yourself, "I can't handle this now, I'm too busy. I'll deal with it tomorrow, next week, or next year." Well, just keep in mind that by the time most people come to me for soul retrieval, they're suffering from physical illness or emotional distress because the lost parts of their soul are demanding to be acknowledged and reintegrated.

The key is to retrieve your lost soul parts *before* they send your life into a tailspin. You can do this by journeying to the Lower World to meet the soul in its own domain. The Laika conceive of lost soul parts as beings that we can engage and speak to, and even heal and rescue. For example, your cruel nature may be personified by a sinister man in a black cape, while your vulnerability may be represented by a frightened little girl.

Now if your soul was fragmented when you were a child, the little girl you retrieve won't just grow up spontaneously. Once that part of your soul is recovered, you need to help her mature and grow up feeling safe. You need to attend to her, nurture her, and make room for her in your life. Sometimes when I help clients, this split-off little girl will speak to me and say, "Why should I come back? This lady says she wants to have more fun and love in her life, but she has no time in her schedule!"

However, if you *do* attend to this soul part, it can grow very rapidly, and your life will definitely change. This is why when a client comes to me asking for soul retrieval, I ask, "Are you sure you have the time and commitment for this right now? Because whatever it is, the change is going to be big. The lost part of your soul is going to follow you home, and it will make you set your life in order again."

But don't kid yourself into thinking that soul retrieval will be like fitting in the last piece of a puzzle that will allow you to solve all your problems—often, it's just the opposite. As a friend once told me, "Healing wrecked my life." Finding the lost part of his soul upset his fragile, unhealthy equilibrium . . . but it also started him on the road to constructing a better life.

Charting the Lower World

Like a traveler who's embarking on a long journey, you first must read the maps telling you where you're going in order to pinpoint your destination. On your first journey, you'll explore the chart of the Lower World, deep within the earth. Remember that although you might think of the Lower World as an imaginal domain that's distinctly different from "the real world," the Laika experience both the literal and the imaginal as real. For the Laika, thoughts, dreams, and visions are just as real as the material world. For the shaman, there is no supernatural world—it's *all* natural, with visible and invisible realms that we can visit through our dreams and imagination. They're as mappable and knowable as our literal world.

Learning the map of the Lower World is akin to an orientation tour of a library, where we learn how to find the periodicals, the literature, and the reference books. We're told where everything is located, but it's only when we begin reading and checking out books that we get to know the true depth and breadth of the place. We discover rare antique masterpieces, the quiet spot in the corner where we can settle in and read, and the vast stores of information about faraway lands. Through journeying, we're able to access the "living library" of our existence, which holds the landscapes, territories, and experiences of our past, present, and possible future. But unlike an actual library, where the knowledge and experiences are safely contained within publications neatly lined up on shelves, the terrain of our lives is mysterious, changing, and experiential.

As you journey, you'll become like the shaman, charting the forbidden and often unknown nooks, fields, crevices, and inlets of the Lower World's mountains and forests. Along the way, you'll begin to sketch the outlines of this landscape into your own map—you'll start to know its contours and uncover some of its secrets, so when you return later to retrieve your lost soul parts and heal your destiny, you'll be able to find your way around. But just as you can have a map of California that gives you the major highways and streets, you can also map the state through hiking trails or by observing the migratory paths of birds. That is, the territory remains the same, but the maps look very different, and the same landscape can have many, many different descriptions.

The map that we're going to work with portrays the soul as divided into four chambers, in the same way that we have a four-chambered heart. In the dreamlike state of consciousness that you experience during journeying, you'll visit these four chambers of the soul and discover the knowledge, wisdom, pain, and gifts inside each of them (this will be discussed in detail in Part II).

I've traced over ancient charts drawn by medicine men and women to create the map you'll be using, and I've explored what may be entirely new trails as seen through modern eyes. But it's important to remember that *the map is not the territory,* in the same way that a postcard from Hawaii won't warm you in the winter. This map is just a tool that will allow you to explore the landscape of your past.

Getting to Lower Earth

The journeying process will lead you through a potent energetic realm. To proceed safely, you must prepare for the voyage by creating sacred space.

In traditional societies, the shaman is protected by her assistants, who remain in prayer while she journeys. The assistants hold sacred space so that the healer's physical form won't be endangered while she's traveling outside her body. Creating sacred space will also allow you to journey safely into the realms of the unconscious—however, please be aware that soul retrieval is a deep process that can elicit unconscious memories that you've been repressing for a long time. (This is why it's especially important that you don't attempt to help someone else with a soul retrieval unless you're professionally trained to do so.)

In ancient cultures, sacred spaces are often associated with temples and ceremonial sites such as Machu Picchu or the Toltec pyramids at Teotihuacán. Many Native American cultures build *kivas* in which to conduct their sacred ceremonies—these are typically circular structures that are built below ground and entered by descending a wooden ladder from the roof. Inside, there's a fire pit, an opening for ventilation, and a small hole in the ground. This hole is called a *sípapu,* and it provides a connection and passageway to the Lower World—access here is a privilege, and it requires the proper training and initiation. When a kiva is no longer used, the sípapu is closed to protect entry to the Lower World.

Although these are all sacred *places,* a sacred *space* can be created anywhere on Earth through the power of prayer. As you set off on your first journey, you'll learn a traditional prayer to create your own sacred space and meet the gatekeeper.

The Gatekeeper

The Lower World of modern man is one that blends all the joy of humanity with all the pain that people bottle up and reject. If the shaman doesn't begin her journey properly, she'll go unprotected and risk being turned away by the gatekeeper, or worse, afflicted by hungry ghosts who inhabit the domains of the ancestors. She can be contaminated by toxic energies and bring them back to the Middle World. So it's important that we respect the rules of the Lower World and those we encounter there, and that we close the door behind us when we leave.

During journeying, you'll imagine your luminous body descending into the Lower World. There you'll meet the gatekeeper of the domains of the soul. This is an imaginal being who guards the entryway to the unconscious, an archetype known by many different names in many different cultures. You'll find him portrayed among early Greeks as the boatman Charon, who ferries souls across the river of death (the River Styx); and as the ferocious three-headed guardian dog, Cerberus. For Tantric Buddhists, the fierce god Mahakala guards the entry to this domain. In the Inka traditions, this gatekeeper is known as *Huascar* ("the one who brings together"), and he's symbolically portrayed as a rope or vine that links the Lower and Middle Worlds. The gatekeeper can be male or female, or both, appearing sometimes as a man and other times as a woman.

When you journey to the Lower World, you'll call out to the gate-keeper, asking for her permission to enter and also for guidance. She's the Lord of Life *and* of Death, the keeper of the seasons, and she calls forth the renewal of the world. She's a luminous archetype that will escort you and provide you counsel during the journey through the four chambers.

You could ask for guides that are familiar, but working with a gatekeeper you're unfamiliar with can be beneficial, because your encounters with him won't carry any psychological or religious bag-gage. Because you'll have no expectations of him, you can have an experience unencumbered by preconceptions. However, you cannot enter the Lower World without his blessing—if you do, you risk getting stuck there, because just as the gatekeeper permits you to enter, he also allows you out. Yet, despite his importance, the gatekeeper has no power to change the journey. Only *you* hold that power.

On your first journey, you'll learn that you can visit a sacred gar-den, a personal Eden in the belly of Mother Earth. As you do so, you'll reestablish your connection to the Great Mother and the feminine.

You'll imagine yourself entering into the earth and traveling down into this sacred garden, washed in sunlight and surrounded by fragrant blossoms and streams. You may visit your personal Eden as often as you like for renewal and healing. Here you'll meet the gatekeeper, who will guide you in the quest for your own Grail.

First, however, you must learn to open sacred space, perform the little-death breathing exercise, and journey to your Eden. (**Note:** Please read through these exercise descriptions several times before you try them.)

Exercise: Creating Sacred Space

First, find a place where you feel comfortable and where you won't be interrupted. Find a nice stuffed chair to sit on, close the curtains, disconnect the telephone, light a candle, and turn on meditative music. In creating sacred space, you'll be opening the doorway between the Middle World in which you live every day and the enchanted terrain of the Upper and Lower Worlds. Through your prayers, you can create sacred space at any location on Earth, and from here you can begin your journey.

To begin, you must first call on the four organizing principles of the universe, which protect you by putting you in proper relationship with all life. The ancients learned that all the poetry of creation is composed with the four letters of the four directions. In biology, we know these as *AGTP*, the four base proteins that make up DNA, the code of life. (Physicists know these four principles as gravity, the weak nuclear force, the strong nuclear force, and the electromagnetic force.) But while science is only able to describe this alphabet, the shaman learns to write poems with it. They call these principal characters "serpent," "jaguar," "hummingbird," and "eagle."

When we connect to these forces from the hallowed ground of sacred space, we're protected, and the organizing principles of the universe respond. This is our agreement with Spirit. When we call, Spirit answers.

To open sacred space, fix your gaze softly in front of you (or close your eyes) and move your hands into a prayer pose at your heart. Extend your hands up with great intentionality past your forehead so that your palms are together above your head. Then reach up to your eighth chakra, which is the soul, and expand this radiant "sun" to envelop your entire body, fanning your arms out to your side. Bring your hands to rest in your lap, and experience the "soul-full" space you've established.

Call to the four cardinal directions of South, West, North, and East, as well as to heaven and earth, and ask them to assist you and protect you. Each point of this imaginal compass is governed by an archetypal animal. In the South, we call to the serpent, which represents knowledge, sexuality, and the healing power of nature. In the West—the land of the setting sun—we call upon the jaguar, the symbol of transformation and renewal, of life and of death. In the North, we call to the hummingbird, which symbolizes the strength and courage to travel great distances and to embark on an epic journey of evolution and growth. In the East, we call on the eagle, which symbolizes the ability to transcend this world. Above us, we call on heaven and the life-sustaining sun, and below us, we call on the earth, the creative feminine.

The following is my prayer for creating sacred space, which you're more than welcome to use. (As you begin journeying regularly, you may wish to come up with your own):

To the Winds of the South,
Great Serpent,
Wrap your coils of light around me.
Teach me to shed the past the way you shed your skin,
To walk softly on the earth. Teach me the beauty way.

To the Winds of the West,
Mother Jaguar,
Protect my medicine space.

Teach me the way of peace, to live impeccably.
Show me the way beyond death.

To the Winds of the North,
Hummingbird, Grandmothers and Grandfathers,
Ancient Ones,
Come and warm your hands by our fires.
Whisper to me in the wind.
I honor you who have come before me,
And those who will come after me, my children's children.

To the Winds of the East,
Great Eagle,
Come to me from the place of the rising sun.
Keep me under your wing.
Show me the mountains I only dare to dream of.
Teach me to fly wing to wing with the Great Spirit.

Mother Earth.
I pray for the healing of all your children,
The Stone People, the Plant People.
The four-legged, the two-legged, the creepy-crawlers,
The finned, the furred, and the winged ones,
All my relations.

Father Sun, Grandmother Moon, to the Star Nations,
Great Spirit, you who are known by a thousand names,
And you who are the Unnameable One,
Thank you for allowing me to sing the Song of Life another day.

Exercise: Little-Death Breathing

Breathing practices are central to many spiritual traditions because they awaken the god-brain, helping us to enter heightened states of consciousness. Patanjali, the author of the yoga sutras, wrote that through the breathing practice of *pranayama,* "the veil over the inner light is destroyed." Here we'll use a breathing exercise called "little death"—just as when you actually die, in this exercise you're going to stop identifying with the ego and experience an oceanic state of communion with Spirit. The little-death exercise produces a heightened state of consciousness necessary for the journey. (Please remember that this exercise is practiced within the sacred space that you've created.)

> *Sit comfortably. Rest your hands in your lap and gently close your eyes or softly focus on a point on the floor in front of you. Inhale to a count of seven. At the end of your inhalation, hold your breath for another count of seven. Exhale in one continuous breath to an additional count of seven, until your lungs feel empty of air. For a final count of seven, do not breathe. Repeat this process seven times.*

Although this exercise sounds simple enough, the "little death" can be disorientating, and you'll probably feel light-headed. This light-headedness is your entry into an altered state of perception, so do your best to hold the full count. I've found this exercise to be as powerful as the states of consciousness I've experienced during deep meditation—it awakens the god-brain and unleashes its capabilities to journey outside of time.

Once you've completed this exercise, proceed with the journey to explore the map of the Lower World.

Exercise: Journey to Eden

Our journey takes us back to our mythical Eden, back to the Mother that we were separated from when we adopted the belief that we'd been cast from the garden. It's an important journey, because even if you weren't raised in a religious home where you learned the myth of Adam and Eve, you *have* been affected by a culture that embraces the idea that we left paradise and can never return—unless we find a secret key to the gate, such as being beautiful, famous, or rich. This will be a sweet journey home, returning to the Mother that has never left us and never will.

This map for the journey is different for every culture, yet it's taught to indigenous peoples from a very early age. Some cultures, such as the Yoruba, follow the roots of a great tree down into the depths of the earth, into the Mother Womb; Arctic peoples imagine that they're diving to the depths of the sea; and rain-forest shamans journey into the depths of the Amazon River. This is your journey to reconnect with the spirit of the earth and the sacred feminine.

> *Imagine your luminous body going down into the earth. Sense the rich, moist soil, the roots of the great trees, and the stones embedded in the dirt. Go down past the bedrock, deeper and deeper, until you find an underground river. Lie down in this stream, sensing the pebbles pressing on your back; and imagine the cool, refreshing water passing through you, washing away any weariness, concerns, or other energies that you may want to shed and not bring with you into the domains of the soul.*
>
> *When you're ready, let the waters carry you deep into the belly of the earth, until you wash up onto the shores of a green, lush garden. Observe a meadow, a spring, and a forest. Find a boulder in this meadow where you can sit and listen to the songbirds. Remember that you can come here anytime you're in need of healing and renewal. This is the life-giving womb of our Great Mother; it's your personal Eden.*
>
> *Call on the gatekeeper: "You, who are known by a thousand names, Lord of Life and Death." Look into the gatekeeper's eyes, and continue: "Keeper of the seasons, allow me to enter your domain. Show me the landscape of my personal Eden."*
>
> *The gatekeeper appears to each of us in a different form—it can be a beloved ancestor, or a religious figure or an angelic being. Allow the gatekeeper to guide you through the groves of trees, lush gardens, and meadows to meet all the animals that make it their home. Enjoy the garden, where you can speak to the rivers and trees and canyons, and nature still speaks to you.*

Once you've explored your personal Eden and discovered its streams, forests, and canyons, make your way back to the shores where you entered, and dive into the waters, allowing them to bring you to the place where you rested before. Relax there once again, letting the waters refresh you as you prepare to return to our world.

Now begin your journey back up through the bedrock, past the roots of the great trees, past the giant boulders, and through the rich, moist soil. Return to the room and into your body. Take a deep breath and open your eyes, feeling fully refreshed and renewed, experiencing the sense of belonging and walking with beauty on the earth that results from discovering that you have never left Eden.

Exercise: Closing Sacred Space

End your journey by closing sacred space, shutting the gateway to the Upper and Lower Worlds.

Bring your hands in prayer to your heart and then open them out to the side. Reaching wide, slowly fan them upward over your head until your palms touch. With your palms touching, bring them down the centerline of your body, to your heart, to the prayer pose. Repeat the prayer to the four directions and heaven and earth that you used earlier, only this time, thank and release each of the spirit animals, and then close sacred space.

Now we're ready to begin the process of soul retrieval. Part II of this book will help you become intimately familiar with the Lower World, so let's get started.

Part II

the LOWER WORLD

CHAPTER FOUR

The Chamber of Wounds

After years of therapy, I thought that I had explored all of my childhood wounds. Instead, I'd only rubbed salt into them so that I could feel something. Last night, I survived the ayahuasca ceremony, but only by the skin of my teeth. If I never do this again, it will be too soon. The old man kept telling me that the funny thing about death is that we all survive it. I felt like my brain was stuck in a crack in the wooden floor most of the night, while I observed my body rotting, the skin peeling off in strips, until I was pared down to raw bone—white, glistening bone—with my brain in between the floorboards. Then all I could see was my skeletal form and images of someone I recognized as myself in Greece, in Pompeii, and in the American Civil War. All different people, but all me—and all being speared, lanced, shot, bayoneted, and left to die a thousand deaths.

"These are the stories that live within you," the old man told me this morning. "Only by knowing all the ways you have lived and died do you exorcise the death that lives inside you."

— from Alberto's journal

Although we traditionally view it as the story of "original sin," the biblical story of Adam and Eve more accurately describes our "original wounding." Genesis tells us that God provided Earth's first man and woman with a paradise in the Garden of Eden. They could do anything they wanted, with one exception: They were prohibited from eating the fruit of a particular tree (the Tree of Knowledge). One day the serpent tempted Eve into taking a bite, and she, in turn, seduced Adam into doing the same.

As soon as they'd succumbed to the temptation of the forbidden fruit, the first humans were cast out of Eden as punishment for breaking God's commandment. Their perfect world was taken away from them, and they were punished with lives of suffering. Eve would suffer pain during childbirth, which is one of the most magical experiences of a woman's life, while Adam would be forced to toil in barren fields. While the Garden of Eden was plentiful with myriad plants and animals to feast upon, only thorns and thistles would now grow for them. When Adam and Eve lost their Eden, their world became a prickly and hostile place . . . as we know, they "fell from grace."

By placing the blame on Eve—who, having been created from Adam's rib, was given second-rate status—this influential Judeo-Christian parable teaches us that it's the fault of the feminine that we're banished from Eden. Eve is the one who's blamed for creating the wound from which we all suffer—the original "mother" wound.

This loss of the sacred feminine that Eden and Eve represent in our culture, whether it's reflected in our disrespect for women or our denigration of Mother Earth, is our *collective* soul loss as human beings. And when we demonize the feminine, we live in a world devoid of the sacred. We end up believing that matter, or the material world, is what's important, not the spiritual. Indeed, the word *matter* comes from the Latin root *mater*, meaning "mother," so in our warping of the sacred feminine, we've come to believe that *things* are maternal, and they'll take care of us. But matter isn't equal to spirit; snapping up Chanel couture is not going to make our spirit soar. Consequently, our divorce from the feminine is the deep, primitive wound we all bear.

Original and Ancestral Wounds

Psychologists interpret this original wounding as the loss of inno-cence that every child experiences in adolescence, a common and necessary passage to adulthood. Mommy can no longer kiss away the hurt, and a child must "leave the garden" and make the transition to self-reliant adulthood, which can be experienced as a personal fall from grace, not unlike that suffered by Adam and Eve. Yet sadly, many children are afflicted with wounds at a time when they're incapable of maturely understanding them. Instead of a wake-up call to adulthood, their wounding results in soul loss. All the child comprehends is that there's pain and trauma in the world, and she's no longer safe.

For example, when a seven-year-old sees Mommy being taken away in a stretcher after an automobile accident, she doesn't understand that this is for Mommy's own good—she thinks that bad people are taking her mother away forever. Such a trauma will cause her to get locked into the emotional response patterns of a seven-year-old, and she'll shut down and pout like a little girl when she's an adult and something she loves is taken from her. She'll continue to look for Daddy (the government, a spouse, or God) to fix the world for her.

Our original wound isn't necessarily the result of a factual event, just like our loss of Eden wasn't a historical event; rather, it's the way things were *perceived through the eyes of a child*. At the time of an injury, all a child understands is that she's frightened and the world has become a dangerous place. This perception is very irrational and very powerful. In fact, it's most likely what makes us succumb to depression, remain in abusive relationships, and stay in jobs that rob us of creative pleasure. We feel that we've been banished from our Eden, so we spend our lives trying to ease the pain that we received during that fall from grace.

We can also suffer from ancestral wounds that have been passed down from one generation to the next—perhaps endured during the Holocaust, the Great Depression, or a revolution. No matter what the cause, we inherit a set of beliefs from our wounded ancestors that we take for our own. Negative attitudes about abundance, scarcity, success, failure, security, sexuality, and intimacy can all come from this ancestral wounding. When this kind of generational soul loss is handed down, children are plagued by issues they didn't even experience in their own lifetimes, yet they end up suffering from despair and self-judgment as a result.

Similarly, we can bring with us a personal wound from an earlier life. Maybe we died trapped in the ice, were banished from our village, or lost someone dear to us—these are all unfinished psychospiritual dynamics that we re-create in this lifetime. And they predispose us to unique "fateful" experiences, much as our childhood traumas do.

The Wounds of Parsifal and the Fisher King

We can see an example of ancestral wounding and how it can derail one's destiny by revisiting the story of Parsifal. You'll remember that his mother, Heart's Sorrow, lost her husband and older sons in battle, so she makes demands on the boy because of her fear of losing her only remaining son. She never wants him to become a knight and suffer the fate of his father and brothers, but what does Parsifal do? He becomes a knight anyway! So his mother begs him to wear a protective garment that she's spun for him, to ask no questions, **and** to respect fair maidens, which doesn't seem like a bad trade-off to the young man. He promises Heart's Sorrow that he'll be good in return for his freedom—but every one of these requests will prevent Parsifal from finding the Grail or experiencing love.

The Fisher King himself can be seen as an external representation of Parsifal's inner wound: He lives in a dreamlike castle and is the keeper of the Holy Grail, yet he can't drink from it because of a wound in his groin. The King's very sexuality is wounded, and he's kept from experiencing the joys of love. He can only be healed when Parsifal asks the crucial question of whom the Grail serves—until then, the Fisher King is living in luxury, but he's still locked outside his garden.

We all know people who've spent their entire lives working to attain material comfort—a big house, an executive position, or some other external manifestation of wealth—only to find that there's absolutely nothing of value in it for them when they actually get what they thought they wanted. Falling into a state of crisis, they divorce and look for a new spouse who they think can make them happy; they may also abruptly quit their job, continue to buy more expensive and outrageous status symbols, or even descend into substance abuse. Living as we do in a highly materialistic culture where people are measured by external marks of success, many of us are like the wounded Fisher

King, incapable of pleasure and forbidden from drinking from the cup of life.

The myth of Parsifal shows us that the only thing of true value—the key to the holiness and joy in our inner sanctums—is making our lives a spiritual journey, an inner quest.

Memories of Eden

Just as we all have a wound from which we suffer, we also have a memory of a Garden of Eden that we yearn to return to—maybe it's our mother tucking us into bed at night, a childhood home, a young love, or a time when our lives seemed carefree. It could even be said that we spend the first part of our lives trying to lose our innocence, and the rest of our lives trying to regain it. This isn't always an easy task—after all, it takes Parsifal an entire lifetime before he can reenter the Grail Castle.

Many of my clients have devoted years to their quest for the Grail, but they've done nothing more than wander aimlessly in the forest of children, jobs, marriages, failures, and successes. They spend years in psychotherapy trying to understand the time they were hurt last, instead of healing the *first* time that they were wounded. They often want to tell me about a recent incident that caused them pain—which I often explain is probably version number 27 of an original wounding that created the beliefs and behavior patterns that are causing them trouble now. *This* is the wound we want to fix, not the 27 later versions.

In fact, there may only be a few major healing themes in our entire lives, all of which stem from our original wounds. The rest of our psychic and physical aches and pains—no matter how devastating—are incidents that express these themes in different narrative forms. They're B movies made from the same script. When we come to understand this overarching theme, we can own it, break free of its plot, and become the authors of our own narrative.

If we continue reliving the wounds that have marked us over and over again, we'll end up passing them on to our children. This is known among the Laika as a generational curse that can only be broken by healing ourselves. When we do, there's a ripple effect that extends forward and backward in time, bringing forgiveness and relief to our children *and* ancestors.

We only suffer when we remain fettered to our past—but the Laika believe that our ancestors suffer as well, until we stop blaming them and heal the wounds they passed on to us. Through journeying, we can identify the original wound and rewrite our ancestral contracts, healing ourselves and charting a course toward a fulfilling destiny. We can then step back into the experience of living in our Eden, and shed the blinders that keep us from fully recognizing that we never actually left.

In contrast to the Judeo-Christian belief that we were born into a perfect state and then banished from it, shamanic mythology says that our perfect nature always remains intact. In fact, other belief systems don't embrace this Judeo-Christian idea of being cast out of Eden—for example, the Aboriginal peoples of Australia weren't cast out; nor were the sub-Saharan peoples, Native Americans, rain forest–dwelling tribes in Brazil, or Pacific Islanders. All of these peoples still perceive themselves as continuing to live in Eden as they speak to the rivers, the trees, and God. In fact, native mythologies go so far as to state that we humans were created to serve and be the stewards of the garden.

While these societies strive to live in harmony with nature (and have done so for millennia), we in the West perceive nature as an adversary to loot and pillage, or as "natural resources" to be consumed at our convenience. We apparently believe that all plants and animals were created to serve and feed man—that all of the food in the world belongs to us. We've justified plundering nature for thousands of years: The great forests in Europe have been clear-cut; we've drilled for oil in the Arctic; and Israel, which is considered one of the most sacred places on the planet by three of the world's great religions, has so polluted its rivers that people have died after falling into the water. This is a far cry from the purification of St. John's baptism. . . .

When a mythology becomes bankrupt, as ours in the West has, a new one must emerge. Today we're looking for new models of sustainability and living ecologically. I believe that these new models will emerge as we journey to heal our original wounding and recover that which we've lost.

Discovering Your Original Wound

To mend your past, you must first enter the Chamber of Wounds and discover the story of your own original wounding—how it happened, who the perpetrators were, when it occurred, and how the story continues to live within you. This chamber contains information about the root of your harmful emotional or health patterns. The memory of this incident is often repressed, so witnessing it again can be extraordinarily soothing by itself. However, traveling to this chamber alone won't heal you—that will happen later. In this chamber, you'll learn the circumstances of your original soul loss, which is just the first step toward healing.

In the Chamber of Wounds, you'll find a kind of play or drama going on that shows the stories that live within you and that choreograph your world. These stories may not be literally true, but they're *emotionally* true. They're subroutines played over and over by the limbic brain. Remember that the unconscious speaks in the language of dreams and fairy tales—in other words, what you find in the Chamber of Wounds may not be what actually happened, but it's how you remember it, and this memory defines the plot of your life. The details of the story are only significant in that they reveal the underlying patterns created by the original wound—the story by itself is of no value (as you'll later come to realize, you're not your stories or your history). But you will be able to engage in dialogue with the figures you find there in order to understand the themes that live in the deep structures of your psyche.

Earlier, I mentioned that the memory of past events may be extremely painful because of our perception of what occurred at the time. For instance, one of my clients suffered from feelings of abandonment because as an 18-month-old child, her parents had left her with her grandparents for a week to seek respite from her colic. Yet in her toddler mind, she perceived that Mommy and Daddy were never coming back, which wounded her deeply.

People who suffer from post-traumatic stress disorder relive painful events as emotional memories throughout their lives, even though the wartime experience or emotional or physical battering occurred long ago. This is because time and clocks don't exist for the limbic brain—so a difficult situation at work can trigger an entire sequence of stress memories, which play themselves out in the synaptic highways of the brain. This is why when we journey to the Chamber of Wounds, we want to observe the event, not reengage it. Reliving a traumatic incident is often more destructive than the incident itself, because by doing so we're forced to repeat painful emotions with no context.

Sometimes the events that continue to cause us emotional trauma are actually from past lives. I recall Sally, a student who discovered a young woman being burned at the stake when she entered her Chamber of Wounds. This woman cried out in a now-obscure Gaelic language, saying that she was innocent and that she loved God. My client interpreted this as a former lifetime of hers in which she was persecuted because she was suspected of practicing witchcraft. Observing this image gave her an immense sense of relief, for she finally understood why she was so irrationally afraid that her family and friends would discover her interests in healing and spirituality. It also explained why she had a phobia of fire—her husband loved to sit by the hearth in winter, but she could only remain by his side for a few moments before leaving with her heart racing.

In soul retrieval, we can change the way we perceived the original event that wounded us, thereby changing all of our future emotional and physiological responses to it—we can actually reroute neural pathways in the brain to elicit joy instead of pain. Thus, when we engage in soul retrieval, we want the benefits to be received at the levels of the spirit, soul, mind, *and* body. We don't just want to bring back an insight that would only be understood intellectually, we want the core transformation of our beliefs, our behaviors, and even our neurophysiology. (After her soul retrieval, Sally was able to openly discuss her interest in energy medicine with her family. She even began to enjoy her time by the hearth with her husband—although she still remains wary of fire.)

My Own Original Wound

Here's a story from my own life, which will give you a sense of the dimensions that soul retrieval addresses:

I was born in Cuba, and when I was ten years old, there was a revolution in the country. War broke out, and no one knew whom the enemy was, since everyone spoke the same language and dressed alike. One day my father gave me his .45 caliber U.S. Army Colt pistol. He showed me how to use it, sitting me down by the front door of our home and explaining, "When I'm gone, you're the man of the house, and you have to protect your mother, sister, and grandmother. If anybody tries to break in, shoot through the door!"

I sat by that door for several weeks listening to gunfire going off blocks away, until three militiamen finally came to the house. At first they knocked on the door, and when no one answered they tried to kick it in. I asked myself, *Do I shoot through the door, or do I wait for them to come inside?* Then I did what any ten-year-old would do: I put the gun down and went to the window. One of the men made eye contact with me through the glass, saw a frightened little boy, and told the others, "Come, there's no one here. Let's go."

That day I lost my childhood. I grew up very quickly during those few weeks sitting with death by the door. I forgot how to just be a kid, and instead became a serious little man. And I also became terrified of strangers—I had recurring nightmares of people breaking down the door to our home and taking all my loved ones.

By journeying, I was able to go back and revisit the boy who faced death when he was ten. In the Chamber of Grace (which you'll visit yourself in Chapter 6), I retrieved little Alberto and told him that everything would be okay, that I'd look after him, and that he was never going to have to be burdened with the survival of his family. When I recovered my 10-year-old self in my early 30s, I got my childhood back. I was able to give up my constant seriousness and mistrust of others, and to stop seeing everything as a life-or-death crisis. I stopped being in survival mode and began to experience the joy of living.

Transformation Through Journeying

While journeying, I unearthed that story from when I was ten, along with many others that I didn't fully understand. I recognized myself as a terrified young man in battle situations; it seemed that I'd relived similar events many times over, lifetime after lifetime. I also learned that familiar themes kept repeating themselves: not trusting my teachers, wanting to hurt the people who loved me, and feeling that every time I met someone I liked, I had to protect them with my life. And all along, I resented my father for making me feel the way I did.

In Native American mythologies, there's a part of us that always resides within God, and a part of God that always resides within us. When we suffer soul loss, we feel that we've become separated from God—that is, we've fallen from grace. When I healed from my soul loss, I recognized that I'd metaphorically been sitting with a gun by the door through many former existences. I continued to identify with and relive an old story line, making me forget my true, infinite nature and my connection to the divine. So it's very important for us to address our soul loss *now*, before our original wounding is passed on to our children, or to the person we'll be born as in our next life.

Soul retrieval allowed me to stop identifying with the story of that ten-year-old Alberto sitting by the door with a gun in his lap ready to shoot any intruders. Through my journey to the Chamber of Wounds, I discovered why that little boy couldn't put down the gun and learn to trust in life and in others. (Later, in the Chamber of Grace, that boy had to learn to trust me, and I had to learn how to live without fear.)

One of my students, Barry, is a stuntman for movies and television. Even though he lost an arm during a childhood accident, he loves performing seemingly dangerous stunts under a very safe and controlled environment. Here's how he described his journey:

> I went down into a pool at the end of the river and met the gatekeeper, a tall, Pacific Islander–like fellow with large brown eyes, who graciously invited me in. To my astonishment, I encountered a

life-size hot dog wearing sunglasses! I wondered what this symbol meant, but all I received was something about "being cool" and "Relax, man" and that I hadn't been relaxed or cool for a long time.

I opened my eyes, and it suddenly became crystal clear: When I was about nine years old, the local kids in my neighborhood used to hang out at the corner hot-dog place. One afternoon I was riding my bike in the parking lot when I was hit by a speeding car that seemed to come out of nowhere.

I was knocked off my bicycle, and although I suffered no serious injuries, an essential part of my energy left me that day. I went from being a very laid-back kid to one who was really uptight with nervous tics. I lost a lot of friends, and to this day have lived more as a "loner." My overall theme on a day-to-day basis has been about trying to predict what's next—trying to see around corners to avoid the next "car." As a result, I think too much and over-analyze everything.

Within months, Barry began to recognize the patterns that kept him from being hurt emotionally, even as he was unafraid of the physical pain of stuntwork. He began to take greater risks in his personal relationships and to discover that the true stunts were performed not in front of a camera, but in the arena of the heart—without a safety net.

Stories and Shadows

You're just about ready to journey to the Chamber of Wounds. Know that this happens in a place of peace and stillness—the more you can find in your own life, the more clarity you'll bring to the journey.

When you find your original wounding, you'll unleash an energy that resides deep within your psyche, as I did when I found the ten-year-old Alberto sitting by the door while a revolution was going on outside. I'd suppressed the memory and had no conscious recollection of that event. Only after my soul retrieval did my father confirm that all this had really happened, and my memory of the events gradually resurfaced. It was then that I was able to understand the aloneness I felt.

In my healing practice, I find that only when we discover our original wound can true understanding follow. In the West, we suffer from what I call "premature evaluation"—the more rapidly we tag something, name it, categorize it, and try to understand it, the more quickly we shortchange the deep transformation taking place.

The original wound you discover in your journey will come to you in the form of a story. When you enter the chamber, you may see a complicated scene taking place in front of you: people shouting at each other, someone having his hand put into a fire, somebody screaming in the background, an old woman knitting, and so on. The beauty of it is that you can go to any of these people and ask, "What's happening here? What's going on? What's the story?" and they'll reveal the way your original wound lives within you, although they may not accurately represent the way it factually happened.

The events you find may also seem unfamiliar because you might encounter soul parts that are so alienated and exiled that it's too painful to recognize them as your own. These are the *shadow parts* of yourself that you shut out, which you often project onto other people. These projections cause you to lash out at others because you see in them the qualities you don't like in yourself. So when you encounter your shadow self in the Lower World (along with the wounds it suffered), you may not recognize it as part of you.

In one of my early journeys, for instance, I remember finding a caped figure whipping a young boy. I assumed that the boy was my lost soul part, but when I asked him, he told me that it was actually the dark man that I'd come to heal. I recall thinking that this was a mistake, that this was someone else's story, for I'd always despised bullies, identifying more with victims. What I realized after my journey was that this bully did not push others around—he bullied *me.* It was my shadow, a part of me that I had to own and heal.

Remember, we all have these shadow parts inside us, even Mother Teresa. Once, when asked why she'd come to Calcutta, she replied that it was because she'd discovered the Hitler inside of her.

Just as our woundings can be ancestral, these shadows or disowned soul parts can also be expressed in the collective realm. For example, Germany had been suffering a period of economic stagnation in the 1920s, but the country's Jewish community was upwardly mobile and was making great advances in music, science, and philosophy. In their stagnation, the Nazis projected their paralysis (their shadow) onto the Jews—and then went on to try to annihilate it. In the process, the Nazis lost their humanity, which is precisely what happens when we lose our soul.

We can also project the positive parts of ourselves onto someone else, or our shadow can be those attributes we wish we had: a shinier, more beautiful, smarter, and more powerful version of ourselves. (This is something that we do all the time in our celebrity-driven culture.)

The author Marianne Williamson has spoken very eloquently about our fear of our lighter nature. When she said, "It is our light, not our darkness, that most frightens us," she was speaking about our need to learn to carry this radiant light within, to feel its powerful and often quite unfamiliar energy. If we're unable to do so, we project this idealized self onto someone else, be it a guru or a teacher, which keeps us from realizing it. This is the reason why a shaman, just like a psychologist or psychiatrist, must have already undergone her own healing journey—so that she can avoid the dangers of projecting her shadow, or her light, onto another.

In the soul-retrieval journey, we'll learn to shine light on our shadow selves so that we can reclaim our disowned selves. As we embark upon this journey, I encourage you to trust the process, and to remember that we're leaving the ordered realm of reason and logic and are entering into the realm of magic and intuition.

Exercise: Journey to the Chamber of Wounds

Prepare for this journey by opening sacred space: Sit comfortably, fix your gaze in front of you (or close your eyes), and take your hands into a prayer pose at your heart. Create the proper intention for this journey, then extend your hands up your centerline very slowly past your forehead, so your palms are together above your head. Then reach up to your eighth chakra and expand this radiant "sun" to envelop your entire body, sweeping your arms out to your sides like a peacock opening its feathers. Bring your hands to rest in your lap.

Call on the four cardinal directions; the serpent, jaguar, hummingbird, and eagle; as well as to heaven and earth. Perform the little-death exercise (inhale and exhale seven times, holding for a count of seven each time), and journey to your garden in the Lower World.

Send your luminous body down into the earth and sense the roots of the great trees. Feel the pebbles and the rich, moist soil as you travel down below the surface. Go past the bedrock, until you find an underground river or stream, and lie in it to rest, feeling the pebbles against your back. Feel the cool, refreshing water as it cleanses you, purifying you for this journey. Allow yourself to be taken by these waters, deep down into the belly of the earth, until they wash you up onto the shore of a sacred garden.

Now stand up and look around. You are entering a garden with a beautiful green meadow before you. Envision yourself surrounded by flowers, and by birds chirping in a nearby forest. Make your way to a boulder by a spring, and sit for a moment to enjoy the verdant beauty around you. This is a place you can come to anytime for healing and renewal.

Now call on the gatekeeper, Lord of Life and Death, keeper of the Lower World, the one who receives the spirits of the ancestors after they have passed and brings them back to the Mother. State your intent to journey into your Chamber of Wounds. The gatekeeper may ask, "Why should I let you into this place where only those who have died may come?" You must state your intent to be shown your original wound, or you won't be allowed to enter. The gatekeeper may say, "Today is not a good day for you to journey." If so, heed his words. The gatekeeper brings harmony to the chaos of the Lower World, and he will know if it is safe for you to enter.

When he lets you in, you must ask the gatekeeper to guide you. To one side, you'll notice a hill with an opening leading into a cavern. Ask that you be guided into this cavern and into your Chamber of Wounds. You have come here to witness the original wound that lives within you, the one that's most crucial for your own healing.

Ask your body-mind to generate an image of what may be in store for you in this cavern. Then step into the Chamber of Wounds and discover the play that's being acted out. You are walking right onstage among all of the players, whom you may or may not recognize. Look into the back of the chamber: Is there a fire? Who's that person in the shadows? What's gathering dust up on the bookshelves? Look about you and explore. If you don't visualize well, try to find another sense that can guide you, whether it be a sense of touch or smell, or even an intuitive sense of what might be going on. This may be more difficult, but at the same time it can be more effective because you won't be distracted by all that visual activity.

The wounded self could be a little boy or girl, a baby, an old person, or even someone of a different gender from yourself. These soul parts are aspects of who you are. Ask your wounded self, "Who are you?" "When did you leave?" and "Why did you leave?" Remember that the wounded self is not the soul part that you're going to retrieve. You'll be bringing back the healed self, whom you'll meet in the Chamber of Grace.

Now prepare to take your leave from this chamber, making your way out the same way that you came in. Take your leave from the Lord of Life and Death. Say, "Thank you for allowing me into your domains, to where only those who have stepped beyond death may come."

Dive into the waters, let them carry you back to where you rested, and wash away any energies that do not belong in the Middle World. Then begin your journey back up through the bedrock; past the roots of the great trees, the giant boulders, through the rich, moist earth; and back into the room. Take a big stretch, rub your hands together, rub your face, open your eyes, and come back into your body. Close sacred space.

Exercise: Journal Dialogue with Your Wounded Self

In your journey, you've encountered some of the stories of your original wounding. In the following exercise, you'll engage in a written dialogue with the central figure you found there, asking it questions to determine the nature of your wounding, as well as what's needed for your own healing.

The journaling process awakens powerful healing voices within the psyche, voices that may not have been heard for a very long time. Remember that until the voice is found, the soul part remains dormant, but once it's discovered, it can begin guiding you back to wellness.

You can initiate a dialogue with this lost soul part on paper. Start by sitting with a journal and a pen in a comfortable place, and open sacred space. When you're ready, draw a line down the center of a blank page. On one side, list the questions you wish to ask; on the other, the voice of your soul part will write the answers. Begin by asking simple questions such as: "Who are you?" but allow enough time for a full dialogue to emerge. Try to continue this process as long as possible, asking your soul part to reveal as much of the story of your wounding as you need to know in order to heal. Also ask this soul part what it needs to be healed—how you can honor it and protect it. Ask it: "How can I make you safe?" "What can you teach me?" "What must I let go of?" and so forth.

When your dialogue is finished, close sacred space.

This process may take several minutes, several hours, or even several sessions.

Now that you've become acquainted with your wounded self, it's time to journey again—this time to the Chamber of Soul Contracts. There you'll learn about the soul agreements you made in the past, along with how you can renegotiate them.

CHAPTER FIVE

The Chamber of Soul Contracts

I came to Peru to experience the ayahuasca and was introduced to death.

Tomorrow I return to the jungle, return to the garden.

Eighty thousand years ago, we acquired a thinking brain: a reasoning machine that set us apart from nature. In one quantum long jump, the brain nearly doubled in size. We could evaluate, reason, think. And the hand of nature was joined by the hand of man.

There is a Gideon Bible in the drawer beside the bed in this hotel room. "And Jehovah God went on to say: 'Behold, the man has become like one of us in knowing good and bad, and now that he may not put forth his hand and take fruit also of the tree of life and eat and live to time indefinite'—with that, Jehovah God put him out of the garden of Eden to cultivate the ground from which he had been taken."

I return to the garden to put forth my hand and eat of the tree of life everlasting. . . .

— from Alberto's journal[1]

"From that day on, they lived happily ever after" is generally what we hear at the end of fairy tales. But when the story doesn't turn out right—when we don't meet the prince, or he turns back into a frog after a few kisses—then "from that day on" becomes a curse. "From that day on, she never smiled" or "He didn't trust" are examples of the agreements we find in the Chamber of Soul Contracts.

Soul contracts are agreements that we enter into in order to survive a crisis, allowing us to cope with painful situations for which there are no apparent solutions. They're the products of the monkey brain, which is willing to compromise everything for a sense of safety. Soul contracts may take the form of promises we make to ourselves ("From that day on, I decided to make a lot of money so that everyone would respect me") or to our parents ("I'll always do everything perfectly so that Daddy will love me"). Regardless of whom we make them with, they keep us repeating the hurts that we discovered in the Chamber of Wounds.

More often than not, these pledges are made silently and honored without discussion—or even consciousness—for many, many years. And although they may have worked well at the time of our wounding to create a sense of security in a world we deemed unsafe, they go on to become the source of our limiting beliefs about abundance, intimacy, love, and success. In other words, a single soul contract will spawn dozens of limiting beliefs.

Although it's often difficult to see the effects of our own soul agreements, we can readily see the effects of such contracts in those around us: The unhappy, driven young man dominated by his father who pushes him to excel in sports, or the awkward young actress with the controlling stage mother who wants her daughter to be a star are both living out a promise to please a parent at the expense of their own calling.

Why We Agree to Soul Contracts

You may be wondering why we agree to such damaging contracts. Again, we look to the Judeo-Christian myth of the Creation for clues. Adam and Eve are cast out of Eden after they eat the forbidden fruit, and from that moment on, their soul contract condemned them to an arduous life that kept Eve submissive to her husband and bound Adam to a life of earning his bread "from the sweat of his brow." Adam,

Eve, and all of their offspring (humankind) were then bound by this agreement to live in exile from Eden, not perceiving the beauty of the world or experiencing the abundance of the garden we live in on Earth. So, their fate was sealed by a contract that affects all of us who have internalized this story.

Imagine how different this contract could have been if Adam and Eve had taken a moment to negotiate a better deal with God. *Negotiate with God? Impossible!* Instead, the first humans walked out of the Garden of Eden in shame, covering their nakedness because it was the best they could manage to come up with.

This is the case with all soul contracts: They're the best we can do at the time because we feel powerless, trapped in a shameful situation that seems nonnegotiable. In this chapter, we're going to learn how every limiting soul agreement can be renegotiated, including those with God. It's now time to explore the obligations we entered into at the time of our original wounding. We need to find out what they say, what terms we've been bound to, and what price we've had to pay for the sense of safety that they provided. Know that there will still be a soul contract when we're finished, but it will be one that we can live with creatively and powerfully, which will allow our healed self to find us within the next chamber.

The Consequences of Poorly Written Soul Contracts

Poorly written soul contracts stunt our development. You'll recall that when Parsifal leaves his mother, she asks him to wear a homespun garment, never to ask questions, and to respect fair maidens. Yet this agreement causes Parsifal to miss out on an opportunity in his youth to live in the splendor of the Grail, and prevents him from consummating a mature love relationship with his soul mate, Blanche Fleur. If he'd allowed his love for Blanche Fleur to blossom, their single night together wouldn't have been chaste . . . but that would have required betraying his mother.

We can't gauge the impact a soul pledge will have on us down the road because we're so consumed by the urgency of the present—Parsifal probably would have agreed to just about anything to get out of his mother's house. We never imagine that the cost will be so high; in fact, we're rarely aware of the cost of our contracts until the price they extract becomes crippling. For example, Parsifal only begins to reckon with his after the hag publicly humiliates him. And even then, he isn't conscious of what's holding him back from a fulfilling life. He only knows that something's missing, but all he can do is what he's always done—until the secret contract is revealed to him.

When Parsifal meets the hermit in the forest, the old man asks him, "Why are you wearing your armor and carrying your sword on a holy day?" At this point, Parsifal is finally forced to confront himself, which breaks the spell. And it's no accident that this is the precise moment that the Grail Castle reappears: When Parsifal reenters the castle and asks the question he'd been forbidden to ask, "Whom does the Grail serve?" the Grail reveals itself to him at last, and he's released from his fate.

Just like Parsifal, many of us get caught in the "warrior phase," spending long stretches in the middle of our lives bound by the terms of soul contracts that demand worldly achievements and success until a health crisis, lost job, or failed relationship forces us to ask, "Why am I doing this?" But by this time, the roles defined in our pledges are the only ones we know. (For example, all Adam knows is tilling the earth until there's sweat on his brow, and all Parsifal knows is fighting.)

So even after we ask, "Why am I doing this?" it may take years before we become conscious enough of our soul contracts to rewrite them. Real change can't occur until we review our obligations and replace old, limiting beliefs with new ones, which allow us to live more meaningfully.

The Myth of Psyche

While the myth of Parsifal is often used to discuss the archetypal path of a man's journey through life, the classic Greek myth of Psyche and her lover, Eros (also known as Cupid), is often employed to examine the development of feminine consciousness. As such, it's an excellent illustration of the archetypal soul contracts that many women face.

Psyche is the youngest and most lovely of a king's three daughters. Her beauty and gentle spirit become legendary throughout the kingdom, and people begin to honor the mortal maiden as a deity. This enrages Aphrodite, the ancient goddess of love and beauty, and she conspires against Psyche, leaving her bereft of suitors. When no one steps forward to ask for her hand in marriage, Psyche's father consults an oracle, which is controlled by the jealous Aphrodite. The oracle condemns the young princess to a marriage with Death. To fulfill this prophecy, her father chains Psyche to a rock, where she's to be ravaged by the most horrible creature imaginable.

Psyche represents the youthful and innocent feminine part of ourselves that's deeply threatening to the old ways, represented by Aphrodite. Psyche wants to be free and to love, but Aphrodite wants her chained to the rock of ages to carry the burden of all the past generations of women. This is a universal myth of the wounding of the feminine perpetrated by one generation upon the next—for example, in African tribes where genital mutilation is still practiced, it's the older women who prepare the young ones for their horrible ordeal.

In this myth, Aphrodite is the equivalent of Parsifal's mother, who saddles her son with the soul contracts that will prevent him from stepping into his becoming. Aphrodite sends *her* son, Eros, to shoot our fair heroine with one of his arrows of love, so as to ignite her passion for Death. But Eros is so taken by Psyche's beauty that he accidentally pricks himself with one of his own arrows and falls head over heels in love with her. With the help of his friend the wind, Eros spirits the fair maiden away to a remote mountaintop. Like for many young women, their father's wish for their betrothal is a fate worse than death—so, condemned to unhappiness, they run away with the first man who promises to rescue them from the tyranny of the parental home.)

The union of Eros and Psyche is pure bliss, but Eros extracts a promise from his lover: She must never look upon him or ask him any questions. This is no different from the husband who demands that his work schedule not be questioned, or that his Saturday golf game take priority over the needs of the family.

For a time, Psyche is happy with this arrangement—her nights are filled with love, and she spends her days eating exotic fruits and being waited upon like a goddess. But, alas, her paradise comes to an end. The serpent energy in Psyche's garden is her two older sisters, who come to visit Psyche in her luxurious mountain abode and become so filled with envy at her happiness that they decide to destroy it. The sisters go to work on Psyche's confidence: They tell her that Eros must be a hideous monster, too ugly to look upon—otherwise, why would he need to extract such a promise from her? They convince her to obtain both a lamp and a very sharp knife to protect herself, and to keep the items in the bedroom so that she can shine a light upon her husband in the middle of the night and cut his throat if she has to.

Psyche listens to her sisters, hides away a lamp and a knife, and then waits for an opportunity. One night after making love with Eros, she rises from their bed, collects the lamp and blade, and shines the light upon her sleeping husband. Psyche is surprised to find not a monster but the God of Love, the most handsome creature in the world.

Seeing Eros for the first time in all his glory, Psyche is so shocked that she stumbles upon one of his arrows and falls deeply in love with him. At the same time, she spills a drop of hot oil from her lamp onto his shoulder. The pain awakens him, and he sees his beloved standing over him with a knife. Frightened, Eros flees—and heads straight back to his mother, Aphrodite.

Brokenhearted, Psyche appeals to the gods to bring Eros back to her, but even they are afraid of the old ways. They all tell her that the only one who can help her is Aphrodite. Psyche doesn't want to ask the jealous goddess for anything, but she feels that she has no other choice.

Psyche's Road to Redemption

By now, Psyche has suffered soul loss twice: First she was betrayed by her father (and not protected by her mother), and then she was abandoned by her beloved Eros. Psyche's visit to Aphrodite symbolizes her journey to the Chamber of Wounds to face the source of her misery. Here she discovers the tasks that will allow her to discard the limiting beliefs that keep her as a weak and suffering girl so that she may become a woman of power and grace.

Aphrodite assigns Psyche four seemingly impossible tasks, promising that if she's able to complete them, she'll be reunited with Eros. The tasks, however, are so daunting that Psyche contemplates suicide at every turn. But the maiden is determined to rewrite her soul contract—she longs to discover her authentic nature, because in the shining light of knowledge, she experienced true love.

As her first task, Psyche is to sort an enormous pile of seeds by nightfall, under penalty of death. (The task is actually not as important as the penalty for not completing it, because we know that the survival of our spirit depends on fulfilling our mission.) An army of ants arrives to help her and saves the day by sorting most of the seeds for her.

Her second task is to cross a river to a field and gather a handful of golden fleece from the powerful rams that graze there. The reeds tell her not to confront the fierce rams directly, but to wait until dusk and gather some fallen fleece from the reeds themselves. Once Psyche has succeeded at this second, seemingly impossible task, Aphrodite assigns her something even more terrifying: Psyche must fill a crystal goblet with water from the river Styx, the river of death. She feels completely overwhelmed by this task, and seriously thinks about taking her life. But then an eagle appears—grabbing the goblet in its talons, it flies to the river, collects the water, and brings it back to Psyche.

The fourth task is the most difficult of all: Psyche must descend into the Lower World and ask the goddess Persephone for a jar of her beauty cream to bring back for Aphrodite. Psyche is terrified by the prospect of entering the province of death, but just as she despairs of ever accomplishing this task, she receives instructions from a mysterious tower. Standing above the earth and representing Spirit, the all-seeing and all-knowing tower advises her to make elaborate preparations for her trip and to follow its instructions very carefully.

The tower tells Psyche that the world she's about to enter is guarded by Cerberus, a ferocious three-headed dog who stands at the gates of the Lower World, barring entry to all but the dead. Beyond those gates, the Lower World is populated by hungry souls desperate for salvation. The maiden is told to carry two coins and two barley cakes, and to say no to those who ask her to come to their aid.

Every other task has been a preparation and a tempering of Psyche's spirit in anticipation of this moment. She knows that she has allies in nature that will assist her, and that she's under the protection of the tower. But now she must journey to the Lower World—the same place to which we journey to meet and recover our lost self—so that she can recover her inner beauty, represented by Persephone's cream.

On her way down to the Lower World, Psyche first encounters a lame man driving a feeble donkey that's loaded down with a parcel of wood. When some of the sticks fall to the ground, Psyche is tempted to bend down and help him retrieve them, but she remembers that she's forbidden to assist anyone and continues on her path. When she reaches the river Styx, she pays the ferryman, Charon, with one of the coins. As they make the crossing, a drowning man pleads for her help, but she refuses him. When they reach the other side of the river, Psyche finds herself on the shores of Hades, where she meets three old women weaving the strands of fate on a loom. They ask her for help, but again she refuses and hurries past them.

Psyche has learned that nothing must deter her from her objective (likewise, we may meet many lost souls in our journey to the Lower World, but must remain true to our intent). Soon, she encounters Cerberus, guardian of Hades. She throws the dog one of the barley cakes, and slips by as his three heads argue over it.

Psyche finally arrives in the hall of Persephone, and following instructions from the tower, she accepts only a simple meal on the floor rather than the banquet she's offered—and it's the sustenance that Psyche requires. (Similarly, when we journey to the Lower World, we may be offered a feast of images, impressions, feelings, and stories, but we must accept only the simplest one that will provide us with essential knowledge.)

Persephone gladly gives Psyche a jar of beauty cream, and the young woman begins her journey home. Yet she can't resist the temptation to peek inside the jar before she leaves the Lower World—when she does, a deadly sleep comes over her, and she falls to the ground in a swoon. (You see, the gifts of the Lower World can't be opened—or deciphered—until we reach our world, otherwise, like Psyche, we can "fall asleep" or become unconscious and miss the true meaning of our gifts.)

Seeing his mortal beloved in danger, Eros comes to the rescue, wipes the sleep from her eyes, and sets her back on her journey. While Psyche delivers the jar to Aphrodite, Eros asks his father, Zeus, for help, and he obliges by allowing Psyche to drink from the spring of immortality. She becomes a goddess, and Eros and Psyche are reunited as equals.

What We Learn from Psyche

This story teaches us that we'll go to incredible lengths to try to live up to the terms of our soul contracts. When Eros rescues Psyche from a marriage with Death, she agrees to whatever he requests of her because he's her salvation. After all, what could possibly be more terrifying than your own father chaining you to a rock to be devoured by a monster? Psyche enters into a contract that requires her to love Eros without really knowing him, and that prohibits her from questioning his identity or his word. She lets him control all aspects of their relationship in order to live in paradise, but she remains unconscious in order to do so. How often women agree to remain oblivious of their own power and wisdom in order not to upset their partner or family!

But we can serve our soul agreements unconsciously for only so long, no matter how complete the paradise—sooner or later, our consciousness will bubble to the surface. Just as Psyche couldn't resist looking upon Eros, our need for self-knowledge brings us into conflict with the restrictions of a soul contract. But as Psyche quickly learns, we can only break the terms with great difficulty, and we'll be launched on a journey that requires us to perform seemingly impossible tasks in order to find what will truly fulfill us.

When we don't rewrite our agreements, we live unconsciously. We rush into relationship after relationship, looking for another "Eros" to rescue us, only to begin the cycle again. For example, shattered by the loss of her husband, Psyche rushes into a new contract with Aphrodite to "save her marriage" rather than courting Eros directly. She agrees to impossible tasks because she views Aphrodite as holding the key to her salvation. Why not just ask the God of Love out for dinner? Once again, she puts her blind faith in someone whom she views as having all the answers to her problems.

The story of Psyche also teaches us about the courage and determination that brings success in the end. It's only after she's crossed the river Styx (which represents that final frontier) and risked danger and death that she finally gains the strength to say no to other people's needs and begins to challenge the terms of her soul contract.

Something has to change, and the first thing to do so is Psyche. As she changes, the whole world changes with her. She sheds her mortal fate and steps into her destiny as a goddess.

Rewriting and Renegotiating Soul Contracts

Many religions recognize the need to renegotiate soul contracts. Judaism has Yom Kippur, a holy day of atonement on which a person not only makes amends for the sins of the previous year, but is also able to release himself from obligations to God and himself that, after sincere effort, he cannot rightly fulfill. Christian absolution is also a renegotiation based on sincere effort, which goes something like this: "I confess that I have sinned. What can I do to renegotiate a contract of eternal damnation?" The penance then sets him on a renewed course that provides absolution.

The problem with religious forms of atonement is that they depend on forgiveness from an outer god or one of his representatives—but through journeying, we can renegotiate our soul contracts directly. We'll sort through what's important and meaningful in our lives, as well as what isn't, as Psyche sorted through her seeds. And, like Psyche, we'll find the golden fleece, the precious wool with which to spin the fabric of a new life, and we'll drink the holy water that few ever taste, before finally going on to the Lower World to recover our inner beauty and strength.

Now, even though awareness of our personal soul contracts is certainly the first step toward transforming them, we don't need to wait for a crisis to begin making changes—we can renegotiate more favorable terms before our world is turned upside down. Often the gatekeeper will assist us, which is exactly what happened to my student Denny:

> My Chamber of Contracts looked like a large legal library: there were many walls lined with books, and there was actually an attendant who took down a book that had my first name on it. I went over to a table and read it. Initially, it seemed to be a listing of all of the attributes that I'd bring into this lifetime. Near the bottom it said, "She or he who is older, bigger, and louder and declares they are smarter, gets to wield all the power." This felt very familiar to me because my older siblings wielded all the power in my childhood. The gatekeeper then started to encourage me in a loving but firm way to move along. Finally, I was handed a large stamp that said "VOID" on it, so I began stamping the word upon this contract with great energy.

When we change our soul contracts, many other aspects of our life will change as well. We'll need to renegotiate the terms of many of our relationships, which some people won't be very happy about. They've become accustomed to our wounded or workaholic self, and as we change, they might feel as though we're letting them down, abandoning them, or disappointing them in some way. We'll need to use our best negotiating skills to rewrite these ancillary contracts as well.

In more ways than we might anticipate, rewriting our soul contracts is a powerful, life-changing experience—so we must let our children, spouses, bosses, and friends know who we're becoming and how they can relate to and support this new, emerging person.

Inherited Soul Contracts

Just as we've inherited psychological wounds from our ancestors, we've also inherited many of their soul contracts. The children of Holocaust survivors, for instance, often suffer deep depression that relates directly to an ancestral contract that's limited their trust and hopefulness in the goodness of the world. Economic fear and a sense of scarcity can also be passed from generation to generation when even one member of a family has suffered through severe hardship, such as the Great Depression. And an inability to trust men can be passed on to a child when a mother is abandoned by her husband.

In such cases, as long as these agreements are in play, present generations get to spend their lives repaying a debt that they know nothing about. Even the Bible speaks of these intergenerational contracts when it teaches that it takes seven generations to repay the sins of the father.

I'd like to share an example of an ancestral contract within my own family. When my brother was diagnosed with brain cancer at the age of 47, I took him to see a renowned healer, who said, "I'm working on your luminous energy field. Within three days you're going to have drainage coming out of the side of your head. Don't take any x-rays, and don't disturb this drainage for ten days." Three days later, like clockwork, a minute opening appeared in the side of my brother's head (which was bald from chemotherapy), and a yellow fluid began to drain out. Nobody could tell what it was.

My father, who was always a skeptic, was quite disconcerted. He panicked and insisted that his doctor order an MRI scan to see what was going on. I begged them to wait out the period requested by the healer. Even the doctor said, "Wait another week—it's not going to hurt you. Medicine can't do anything for you anymore."

Although he'd exhausted all of his Western-medical options, my father's concern won out. When the MRI was done, the drainage stopped—and my brother died two weeks later.

It's true that my brother had to make a choice to reevaluate his soul contract that said, "If I disobey my father, he won't love me." But given his weakened state, he didn't have the energy to do so, even though he'd been struggling his entire life to break free of this pledge. My brother ended up protecting his soul contract with his life because he didn't want to betray or disappoint our father—it was easier to accept death than to change his beliefs.

Reluctantly, I had to accept my brother's choice and help him as best I could, but I always felt that it didn't have to end this way.

Rewriting or tearing up a soul contract is a liberating force that allows us to develop open-ended belief systems that lead us to new life experiences and new agreements, possibly even saving our lives in the process.

A Mother's Promise

One of my clients, Bonnie, received a call out of the blue from the daughter from whom she'd been estranged for a number of years: Doctors had found a lump in her breast, and she was scheduled for a biopsy. Rather surprisingly, it seemed that the young woman wanted her mother to be with her.

Bonnie called me to say that she'd been crying uncontrollably since speaking with her daughter. "It's not sadness; I don't know what it's about," she said. Since she had to accompany her daughter to her biopsy appointment on Monday and then follow that up with a grueling day of meetings at work, she was so overwhelmed with emotion that she feared she'd be unable to be much good in either situation.

I met her late on the Saturday before the biopsy, and we journeyed together. In the Chamber of Wounds, she found herself as a young mother living in a medieval cottage with her two babies. They were being terrorized by marauders, who had knocked down one of the support beams of the house. The mother and her babies were trapped under the fallen timbers of the cottage, and she knew that they wouldn't be able to escape. It was wintertime and the sun was setting, and she knew that they were all going to freeze to death. She was in terrible pain, but she kept reassuring her little ones, "It's okay. Mommy's here."

In the Chamber of Soul Contracts, Bonnie found herself asking God to take her children before she died so that they could hear her comforting them. This soul contract ("Let my children die before I do") was centuries old, but it was still in force. It was a terribly worded contract with horrifying results—but in times of crisis, we do the best we can.

Bonnie's ancient soul contract was affecting her response to her daughter's biopsy. During our soul retrieval, she was able to renegotiate this agreement, changing its wording to: "Let my children know that their mother will always be there to comfort them."

My client stopped being emotionally shaken as soon as she understood the events that were causing her grief. She realized that she'd pushed her daughter away because she couldn't bear the thought of losing her. Within days, the biopsy showed the lump in her daughter's breast to be benign, and Bonnie's relationship with her daughter began to mend.

In Bonnie's case, we see how a soul contract can be carried from one lifetime to the next and activated by a crisis. In the case of Linda, we'll see how a soul contract from *this* lifetime can be rewritten.

The Smoke Cleared . . .

When I met Linda, a successful corporate coach and accomplished photographer, she'd been diagnosed with breast cancer and was undergoing chemotherapy. In her Chamber of Wounds, we discovered a frightened and angry three-year-old child. When I tried to approach this little girl, she ran away crying, saying that she couldn't trust anyone because they'd leave her.

Linda recognized this child and explained, "In a way, I was completely abandoned by the time I was three. Mother was hospitalized with postpartum depression at my birth and wasn't present for months; then my father was killed when I was 18 months old. Mom and I went to live with her parents, and when I was small, I saw my grandmother almost set herself on fire trying to ignite the pilot light in the oven. After that, I decided she wasn't a safe refuge . . . but my grandfather was tender and strong. I have a wonderful memory of him lifting me up to look through the rectangular openings in a high wall. I could see a secret garden on the other side, and was thrilled. He also made me a book of songs and poems I still have. He died in his sleep when I was three years old, and a part of me left, too.

"The soul contract I made," Linda continued, "was to stay in the shadows. I made the decision to create alone, to play alone, and to not go out into the world."

When we passed into the Chamber of Soul Contracts, Linda saw an ancient cliff covered with petroglyphs that were partially obscured by black smoke. The smoke had protected her from reading this message until she was finally ready to accept it. She asked the smoke to clear, and as it did, she could see that the petroglyphs spelled out the word *YES*. "That's my new contract," Linda realized. She was being asked to say yes to life and the opportunities it presented to her.

"All of a sudden, the moment became very serious, for I knew that this was a spiritual vow I was being asked to take," she said. "If I didn't say yes, the opportunity might not arise again. If I did, I'd better live it. I could feel and sense that it was big. I was scared, but I also felt blessed—so I said yes."

As you can see, these contracts carry a huge price. In my brother's case, it claimed his life. Bonnie spent many years alienated from her daughter and without a significant romantic relationship in her life; however, a year after her soul-retrieval journey, I performed the wedding ceremony for her and her new husband. Linda's health and creativity were compromised until she renegotiated these contracts and could start saying yes to life—now she's in remission from cancer and is back to being a gifted artist and coach.

Exercise: Journey to the Chamber of Contracts

As before, prepare for this journey by opening sacred space. Sit comfortably, fix your gaze in front of you (or close your eyes), and take your hands into prayer pose. Focus on your intention to enter the Chamber of Soul Contracts. Reach up to your eighth chakra and expand this radiant "sun" to envelop your entire body. Call on the four cardinal directions to open sacred space. Perform the little-death exercise, and journey to your garden in the Lower World.

When you greet the gatekeeper, state your intent to explore the soul contracts you've entered into. He will guide you from your garden into your Chamber of Contracts. When you're there, look about you, and engage in dialogue with the characters you meet. Ask questions: "Who's that person by the fire? Who's sitting in the rocking chair? What's the scene that's happening around me? Who are the characters?"

You may meet yourself at the age you were when you entered into that contract, and he or she will explain what you agreed to; or perhaps you'll find a self from a previous lifetime. You may even find an ancestral contract and the person who first negotiated it. Ask the following of whomever you find: "What are you writing on that board?" "What are you scribbling in that notebook?" and "What are you repeating to yourself?" Remember that every contract assures you of something (safety, love, relief) in exchange for something else (the price you pay). What price are you paying, and what are you getting in return? Is it really worth it? Ask this figure, "What is it that you really want?" "What is it that would bring you peace or comfort or safety?" and "If you could ask God for anything, what would it be?"

Explore the language of the contract. If you need help, ask the gatekeeper, an all-knowing figure, to explain it to you. Then propose more favorable wording. Keep trying until you come to a new agreement that's positive and life-affirming.

Before you go, explain the new contract to any other people in the chamber. By doing so, you are installing this contract into your unconscious so that it's effective immediately. Tell the people you've found: "You don't need to be doing this anymore. That script is not being performed here any longer. It's complete; it's done. You can be at peace now. Here is our new agreement." Be sure that all of the characters in this drama know that this theater piece has come to an end. Reaffirm this new soul contract with each one of them so that they're fully informed of the new agreement.

Now make your way out. Take your leave from the gatekeeper, Lord of Life and Death. Tell him, "Thank you for allowing me into your domains, to where only those who have stepped beyond death may come."

As before, make your way back to our world. Take a big stretch, rub your hands together, rub your face, open your eyes, and come back into your body. End your journey by closing sacred space.

Exercise: Journal to Renegotiate Your Soul Contracts

The second chamber reveals the soul contracts you entered into at the time of your original wounding, and you've just asked the figures there to explain the details of your agreement to you. Now you can use the journaling process to renegotiate your contract and obtain more favorable terms that will cease constricting you in your everyday world.

The journaling process awakens the voices of powerful healing elements within your psyche. This is the voice of the soul part that seeks a new, life-affirming agreement with you. Start by taking your journal and a pen, and getting comfortable in a place where you can open sacred space.

When you've done so, draw a line down the center of a blank page. On one side, list the questions you'll be asking; on the other, write the answers given by your soul part that seeks to establish a new contract with life. Begin by asking simple questions, such as "Who are you?" "How have you come to help me?" and "What is it that you really meant to ask for?" Transcribe the dialogue onto paper—through it, you'll further establish the terms of your new soul contract. Allow enough time for a full conversation to emerge.

The following is an example of Bonnie's dialogue as she renegotiated the terms of her soul contract:

> **Bonnie:** Why are you crying?
> **Woman:** The smoke, I can't see my babies . . .
> **Bonnie:** Where are they?
> **Woman:** Under the rubble. I can hear the little one crying. . . . God, why have you done this to me?! Let them die before I do, so they can hear my voice and know that I'm here with them.

Bonnie: Is that what you really want to ask God for? Don't you mean to let your babies know that their mother is there for them, and that she loves them?

Woman: I don't want them to die alone.

Bonnie: Try this: "God, let my babies always know that I'm with them and I love them." Is this what you mean?

Woman: Yes, that's what I want. Let my babies know that Mommy is always by their side when they need her.

Bonnie: Be at peace, my dear one. It's okay to go home. Your babies are well.

Now here is Linda's conversation as she renegotiated the terms of her soul contract through the figure of her grandfather:

Linda: Where are you?

Grandfather: I am all around and inside you.

Linda: I'm sorry I haven't been aware of you. I thought of you as my literal grandfather, who left long ago. How do I begin to recognize you?

Grandfather: I'm here now, and I was here long before your literal grandfather was born. You've seen me in the tree at the foot of the driveway. You've felt me blow in on the winds of the storm. You've heard me, an owl, at night. You've sensed me in the land, in the legends and spirits of the people who lived here before you. Once you start looking, you'll see me.

Linda: That's so very beautiful—thank you. I need your strength now, your protection. I'm trying to grow, to integrate the flame inside, the wisdom. It's all huge, and my smaller self is afraid and still vulnerable.

Grandfather: I have watched these things and consider them as precious as a fragile plant emerging from a seed. Yes, you *are* vulnerable, but the plant is alive, rooted, protected, and watered by the rains of Spirit.

Linda: How can I call on you to shelter and protect little Linda?

Grandfather: Call on me every day in your meditations, and we'll speak to one another. I will touch you, and you'll feel my arms around you. I'll lift you up to look through the openings in the wall, and you'll see the secret garden on the other side. One day you'll live there, but first it will be your job to lift others to look through the opening so that they may see that the garden exists.

Linda's new contract brought her a mandate to "help others see the garden." Her new contract made it clear that her healing was closely related to the healing of others.

Exercise: Journal Dialogue with God

We can also renegotiate our ancestral soul agreements with God— after all, why should we simply settle for a pact that was made on our behalf by an ancient ancestor? There are many examples of renegotiated contracts with God in the Old Testament. In the story of Sodom and Gomorrah, for example, God says to Abraham, "I am going to destroy these two cities, because people no longer keep My ways." Abraham asks God, "If I can find 50 righteous men, will You spare these cities?" God says, "Yes." Abraham comes back to God, and says, "What if I can only find 45 righteous men?" God says, "Yes," He will spare the cities. Abraham asks, "What if I can only find ten righteous men?" And God again agrees that He will spare the cities. This is the end of Abraham's negotiations.

When the angels go to Sodom, they find only one righteous man, Lot, and they urge him to take his family and flee before the city is destroyed. We'll never know what the outcome would have been if Abraham had requested God to spare the cities if he found only one righteous man. In negotiating the contract, Abraham also could have said to God, "Spare my people, for *I* am a righteous man."

Try this dialogue with God to discover how this ancestral contract of being cast out of the garden and condemned to a life of shame and suffering lives within you, and how it can be different. First, open sacred space, and draw a line down the middle of a page in your journal. On the left side, you'll write your questions, while you'll record God's answers on the right.

Begin by asking God, "What happened back then?" "What did Eve do?" "Who was the serpent?" "What did Adam do?" "What part of me lives in shame?" "Where does suffering live within me?" and "I see You everywhere I look and feel You in every cell in my body; will You walk by my side?"

End by closing sacred space.

Make your dialogues with God a daily practice.

Now that you've renegotiated your soul contract, this new agreement will guarantee your healed self the safety it requires to meet you in the next chamber.

CHAPTER SIX

The Chamber of Grace

My father died at the age of 50, although he lived to be 76 years of age. . . . He died the other death, the one that robs us of our spirit and leaves us devoid of life. I promised myself to die differently.

I know that the power that one may acquire on the journey of the Four Winds is made of more than knowledge gained, epiphanies of spirit, responsibility felt, and the skills to become a caretaker of the earth. It is also the acquiring of different lives.

There is an energy body. One acquires this in the South.

There is a nature body, an etheric body that one acquires in the West. The body of the jaguar.

There is an astral body, one that has the lifetime of the stars. This is in the North. The body of the ancient masters. A mystical body. Wisdom of the universe.

There is, I think, a causal body in the East. The thought before the action. That which exists before the fact. Creative principle. The eagle body.

So here I am, knowing that I must continue my journey. There are new questions to be answered. There are experiences yet to be served. . . .

— from Alberto's journal[1]

When we're in the state of grace, we're fully animated by life. It's what the Chinese call "awakened chi," or what makes us bound out of bed in the morning and allows us to overcome the obstacles of life. When we've fallen from it, however, greeting the day is a chore, and everyday life is a burden to be shouldered as best we can.

Even though our soul seeks to live in grace, we usually only take note of it when we feel its lack—for example, when our life force is exhausted from an abusive marriage or work situation, or when we're pressured to compromise our dreams by following a course in life that's expected of us but is far from our heart's calling. It's then that we become addicted to quick hits of that elusive elixir known as "happiness."

Grace Versus Happiness

Most of us confuse grace and happiness, but the former is profound and transformative, while the latter is fleeting and causal. In Western industrial society, we're at the mercy of the alignment of favorable circumstances for happiness, which is far from the innate sense of well-being we know as grace. We're so hooked on this notion of happiness being brought about by events or circumstances that we're perplexed by the contentment of "simple" or "poor" people—those with no more than the food in their belly, a roof over their head, and the good health of their children and loved ones, for instance.

Research shows that the variance in happiness between those who are struggling to find their next meal and those who are able to provide for their basic needs (such as food and shelter) is quite substantial, yet there's little difference between those who have their basic needs met and those who are extremely wealthy. Sure, the expensive car or fancy dress works for a while, but we adapt quite quickly and our latest toy becomes the new norm—thus, we're thrown back into a state of desire. To paraphrase the words of Aldous Huxley, we make the ceiling of yesterday's desire the floor of today's expectations.

Just as Chinese medicine looks upon an obese person as someone who's actually starving to death, desperately trying to fill a hole in their being with food, we can also think of the compulsive spenders among us as frantically trying to purchase a cure for a psychological or spiritual void in our lives. By lacking a sense of inner peace, we stumble through the motions of life without ever truly living in the moment, and we try to satiate uncomfortable feelings by throwing money away, overeating, taking on serial sexual partners, or working obsessively. Or we may fall into substance abuse, which provides only fleeting moments of happiness that vanish quickly and leave us feeling even more depleted.

People dabble in narcotics for the sensation of getting high, but when dependency sets in, that high is replaced by a pernicious sense of deprivation. We call an addiction "having a monkey on our back" for good reason: When humans fall prey to the instincts of the monkey brain—fear, feeding, fighting, and fornication—our existence becomes a fight for survival, making it impossible to live in grace. The two are mutually exclusive. In grace, you're free to be like "the lilies of the field" who need nothing, or those who "walk in the valley of the shadow of death and fear no evil" . . . but momentary pleasures can't and won't bring us this state. After all, what better image of grace is there than a baby's smile? Babies don't strive for happiness or brace themselves against sadness, they just *are*. That's grace.

Moving from Fear to Grace

Loss of grace brings about fear, causing us to enter into survival mode. And when we feel that our survival is threatened, we create a "Plan B." For example, two weeks before my son was born, I went into a frenzy: "I've never been a father in my life! I don't know how to do this!" I screamed to myself. "I'm pretty good in the Amazon, but I know nothing about parenting!"

I was frightened by the idea of driving a minivan and becoming a soccer dad for the rest of my life when I'd always been an explorer. So I told myself, "Well, if this doesn't work, I can always go back to the rain forest." This was my Plan B, an escape hatch I kept open that prevented me from being fully present for my family. When I realized what I was doing, I closed that hatch and burned my Plan B. I became determined to make "Plan A" the only one that I'd endorse. In fact, shortly after my son was born, I enjoyed two years of being the primary parent while his mother went to medical school.

Burning our Plan B—our fear plan—allows us to free ourselves from wasting a tremendous amount of psychic energy that we can reinvest in Plan A. As simple as this sounds, it's the criterion for recovering grace, because grace and fear cannot coexist within the same plan.

The Fisher King and Grace

In the myth of Parsifal, we come across the wounded Fisher King, a classic example of someone who's cut off from his grace. When we first meet him, the king is living in the Grail Castle, moaning in pain as he lies on his litter, suffering from a wound in his groin while the lively court celebrates around him—including knights and fair maidens eating, dancing, and drinking from the Grail. Yes, the Fisher King lives in the presence of the very thing that can heal him, but he can't partake of it. (This is how it is with grace lost: We're surrounded by beauty but are unable to recognize or enjoy it.) Instead, the king must suffer and wait for the off chance that a naïve young lad such as Parsifal will stumble into the castle and ask the healing question: "Whom does the Grail serve?"

The Fisher King represents the wounded self that we carry within us for much of our lives. We observe joy and beauty all around us, yet we prohibit ourselves from being part of it. The mature Parsifal also ages into a version of the Fisher King—he still performs his knightly duties, but without joy. The fire that burned within him as a youth is all but extinguished. He wanders aimlessly throughout the countryside, forgetting that he's waiting for the reappearance of the Grail Castle. Jaded and bereft of his innocence, he spends his life doing what he's always done—rescuing fair maidens and freeing castles under siege—until he's asked to remove his armor. When he finally rediscovers the Grail Castle and asks the critical question, both Parsifal and the Fisher King heal simultaneously, allowing them to receive the grace of the Grail.

Now the reason that the Holy Grail was never found by any of King Arthur's knights except Parsifal is because it doesn't exist in the physical world—it only resides in the invisible Grail Castle. This is a place that all the wisdom traditions say can never be found by seeking . . . yet can only be discovered by those who seek. In other words, we have to embark upon a quest to find what has always been available to us or we'll pass this task on to our children.

You see, Parsifal and the Fisher King are both aspects of ourselves: If our Parsifal never finds the Grail, he becomes the Fisher King, hoping and praying for someone to heal him. I often see this as a wound that's passed from mother to daughter, or from father to son: The parent was never able to heal or save the Parsifal within, so he or she passes the wound on in the hopes that the next generation will heal it for all who came before.

Ultimately, all soul loss is a separation from our own divinity, from our natural self that always lives in grace. This self doesn't reveal its face until we confront our wounds, have the courage to rewrite our limiting soul contracts, and begin the hero's journey toward healing. We imagine grace as some kind of divine state that we can enter if we just practice the right type of meditation or say the right prayer. But there's no road sign that says "Grace thataway," pointing to the route that leads us there.

Observing our original wound, as we've done in our earlier journeys, provides great insight: Many of my clients are relieved when they finally comprehend that their phobia of fire, heights, or confined spaces comes from an experience in a former lifetime. But deep healing requires that we go beyond insight to renegotiate the contracts made by our wounded self, and that we then recover our healed soul part.

Parsifal wandered through life for years before reentering the Grail Castle; Psyche had to undergo a profound loss of innocence and four seemingly impossible tasks before she could find that inner beauty that supported her not only as a child bride but as a goddess. There's just no way to recover our grace without embarking on a hero's journey. To do so, we must go to the Chamber of Grace to retrieve that soul part that always remained in grace. It's here that we'll discover our healed self, which has been kept in a state of harmony. What we'll recover, which we bring with us on our return to Eden, is born of wisdom: It allows us to trust again shrewdly, to love again sagely, and to live heartily.

Lisa's Heroic Journey

When I met Lisa, she was 45 years old and battling a severe form of leukemia, caused by inherited chromosomal damage. She was terrified by the severity of her illness and traveled to Houston from Los Angeles every three months to monitor her condition.

When we performed her soul retrieval, Lisa and I found that her Chamber of Wounds was a gloomy space shrouded in darkness. In the shadows, we discovered a statue of a woman with a knife in her heart, and she wouldn't speak or respond to us in any way. When we went into the Chamber of Soul Contracts, there was a note written on a blackboard that said: "I'd rather die than live with loss." We continued our journey and entered the Chamber of Grace, where we found a young girl sitting on the floor playing jacks. She smiled at us and continued her game.

Very shortly after getting her cancer diagnosis, Lisa had begun questioning her aunt about her childhood, and she discovered a traumatic story from her past. When Lisa was 19 months old, her father stabbed her mother to death and then knifed Lisa and her four-year-old brother in the chest. The next day, the police found the children bleeding next to their slain mother; their father was found dead several days later, having committed suicide.

Lisa had no conscious memory of these events for the first 45 years of her life. She knew nothing about how her parents had died, even though she and her brother both had scars below their hearts from their father's attack. She'd always considered the aunt and uncle who raised the two children to be her parents, and accepted that what had happened to her biological parents was a deep, dark secret, not to be discussed. She even believed that the scar below her right breast was a birthmark. It was evident that Lisa was in denial about this incident.

What had happened to her was too terrifying for a child to under-stand—it was even too horrific for an *adult* to comprehend.

It wasn't until my client's soul-retrieval journey that the realiza-tion of that wound forced itself upon her. That night, Lisa awoke with the sensation of being stabbed in the heart—she was in anguish like she'd never experienced. Seeing the statue with the knife in its chest triggered a memory that caused her physical pain, and she was reluctant to return to the Chamber of Wounds, fearing that she'd be overwhelmed by grief (even the Chamber of Contracts seemed too dramatic and intimidating). Lisa had seen her original wound, and her body remembered . . . she knew that her soul contract related to her heart being wounded. In a symbolic replay of this childhood incident, she'd even had the catheter through which she received her chemo-therapy placed right next to her heart—an open hole over her heart, with a tube leading to it.

In physics there's a theory of "critical point analysis," which states that you ought to work where the least amount of effort will have the greatest effect. To that end, I knew that we needed to experience the positive life force represented by the girl playing jacks whom we found in Lisa's Chamber of Grace before we could revisit her Chamber of Wounds.

Immediately after the soul retrieval, I had Lisa play an imaginary game of jacks, first picking up 1, then 2, then 3 jacks, and so on, prodding her onward until she picked up all 12. She struggled with imagining the game as it got more and more complex, but jacks was a perfect game for Lisa. It required skill, dexterity, and concentration, but the game is entirely noncerebral. As the game increased in complexity, her usual need for control had to be set aside. After the final round, when she'd picked up all the imaginary jacks, she had a big smile on her face.

This exercise helped Lisa embody her young and unwounded soul part. She did so by extending her hands and welcoming the little girl who was filled with grace into her heart chakra, and feeling that child's energy infusing her entire body. The game also allowed her to understand that she had the skill and instinct to do well in jacks—and in life.

After the game, we journeyed back into the Chamber of Wounds and faced the statue with a knife in its heart. Despite the obvious reference, Lisa still couldn't understand why this statue was there. All she knew was that she was paralyzed in its presence. I asked her to grab the knife from the statue's heart and draw it out. Suddenly, her arms began to move and she realized that she could withdraw the knife that was still symbolically and energetically wedged in her own heart.

A few months later, Lisa went back to Houston for a checkup and found that her leukemia was in remission. It has never returned.

Receiving the Lost Soul Part

While working with Lisa, I visited the Chamber of Grace before returning to the Chamber of Wounds—a common practice when someone has suffered from a huge trauma such as Lisa had. I knew that she needed the fortitude to face a very difficult situation, and in a case like this, it was important to visit the Chamber of Grace several times and reassure the lost part of Lisa's soul that she was ready to receive her. If she'd brought back her vulnerable soul part without creating a nurturing and safe environment for it in her life, it would have gone right back into exile because she couldn't welcome it and integrate it into her world.

As you can see from Lisa's story, what you encounter in the Lower World can be very upsetting. At The Four Winds Society, where I train students to practice healing through soul retrieval, I insist that they master this technique before practicing it on someone else. It's very important to maintain great integrity and focus when you retrieve a lost soul part, but it's particularly true when journeying on behalf of another person—it's a delicate process that requires restraint.

Can you imagine how hard it is for a wolf to bring back a delicious rabbit for a wounded member of its pack from miles away, carrying it in its mouth without eating it? Similarly, a soul part is a delicate and rich portion of energy that can be tempting for practitioners to use for their own healing, instead of for the healing of someone else. An unhealed guide may project his shadow onto the person he's supposed to be helping.

Remember, when you enter the Chamber of Grace to retrieve a lost part of your soul, you'll have to reacquaint yourself with that soul part and protect her. (You'll learn how to do this through the journal exercise at the end of this chapter.) Finding an original wound won't produce grace, nor will renegotiating a soul contract—*you need to retrieve the lost soul part and take its energy and emotional resources into your chakra system* so that it can reinform your neurophysiology and your brain. Only this will allow you to again experience safety and grace.

After your visit to the Chamber of Grace, you can't just expect to suddenly jump to the happy ending and live in joy and grace for the rest of your life. Grace is a hero's journey that begins in this chamber, and it commences at the energetic level when you absorb the soul part in through your chakra system. Fortunately, the soul part will instruct you and guide you through the tasks you must perform to receive it and welcome it home.

Exercise: Journey to the Chamber of Grace

Prepare for this journey by opening sacred space. Sit comfortably, reach up to your eighth chakra, and expand this radiant "sun" to envelop your entire body. Perform the little-death exercise, and journey to your garden in the Lower World.

When you greet the gatekeeper, state your intent and ask to meet the self that has remained whole and in a state of grace. This might be a young girl or an old man or a middle-aged woman. Ask questions such as: "Who are you?" "What gifts do you bring to me?" "How do you trust?" "How do you play?" "How can I look after you and protect you?" and "What parts of me must change in order for you to remain with me?"

Ask the soul part if it is ready to come back with you. Sometimes it will give you a list of things that you must do before it is willing to return. For instance, it might ask, "Why should I?" and point out that you have no time for its innocence, joy, and play. Sometimes it will tell you to return for it in a week, after you have cleared up a relationship in your life, giving you a seemingly impossible task like the ones assigned to Psyche. Often it will give you a to-do list of beliefs, attitudes, and behaviors that you must change in order to embark on the hero's journey.

Invite your soul part to return with you if it is ready. Go back to your garden, calling on your soul part to join you. Thank the gatekeeper and dive into the waters, allowing them to carry you to where you rested. Journey back into your room and your body.

Next, reach out with your hands and invite the soul part to enter your body through whichever chakra your instinct guides you to. Receive it with the palms of your hands and bring it to your chakra. If you are not sure of which chakra your soul part belongs in, bring it to your heart chakra at the center of your chest. Take a deep breath, and feel the essence of your missing self filling every cell in your body with its power and grace. Take another deep breath and know that you'll never be separated from yourself ever again. Then close sacred space.

Exercise: Personal Affirmation

It's helpful to develop a personal prayer that reaffirms that you walk through life in a sacred yet playful manner, seeing and appreciating the beauty that surrounds you, and reaffirming your place within that beauty. The following prayer, which is based on a traditional Navajo poem, is a personal mantra that I use in my daily life to inform my world and maintain my grace. I'm happy to share it with you:

Beauty before me,
Beauty behind me,
Beauty around me.
I am surrounded in beauty.
In beauty I walk.

My personal prayer reaffirms the gifts and grace of my healed self. There's nothing as great as the power of prayer, particularly when it's yours and from the heart.

As you develop your own prayer, make sure that it's a positive affirmation. It shouldn't be a request for something to be given to you or for something to be fixed—instead, it's an expression of appreciation for life itself, a tool to nurture your grace and restore bliss. Repeat this prayer regularly, as if adding water to a plant. Once recovered, grace must be cherished and nurtured so that it propels you forward and brings you joy and peace.

Another personal prayer, which you can repeat in the morning when you wake up and throughout the day, is:

Mother Earth, Father Sky
Thank you for the beauty and love that surround me.
May I bring peace to myself, and everyone I touch,
Joy to myself, and everyone I see.
I walk in beauty, joy, and peace.

Open sacred space and take some time to voice your own prayer. Write it down and hold it in your heart.

When you're finished, close sacred space.

Exercise: Journal Dialogue with Your Newly Recovered Soul Part

This journaling dialogue will help you understand your lost soul part so that you may integrate her into your life. You may notice after doing this dialogue exercise that your soul part begins to visit you in dreams or in visions as you're meditating.

As before, start by opening sacred space, and then draw a line down the center of a blank page of your journal. On the left side, write questions for your lost soul part to answer on the right side of the page. Your questions might include: "How can I protect you?" "What lessons do you have for me?" "How can I make your world safe?" "How can I honor you?" and "What are your gifts to me?"

Allow the dialogue to flow—don't rush.

Close sacred space when you're finished.

CHAPTER SEVEN

The Chamber of Treasures

*Everyone seems to think that I am an anthropologist, yet in
my heart I know that I am a poet.*
— from Alberto's journal

If Billie Holiday had never learned to use her soul-stirring voice to
record her struggles against racism, or if Anne Frank hadn't poured
out into her diary her harrowing tale of hiding from the Nazis, their
suffering would have overwhelmed their lives—and the entire world
would have been impoverished by the loss. Instead, each woman used
her gifts to overcome daunting circumstances and launch herself into
her destiny.

Extraordinary as these examples are, every single one of us has gifts:
treasures that we can bring up from the Lower World that will lead us
to our destiny. Unfortunately, many of us are unaware of these hidden
capacities because we've settled into the lifestyle required of us by family, work, and circumstance. We get on a "train through life" and stay
on it, regardless of whether it's the right one or not. We stay on board
simply because we've found a seat and it's too much trouble to pick up
our baggage and change at the next station. For example, in college
we take an aptitude test that indicates that we have a talent for a career
in medicine, when all our soul wants to do is design airplanes. So our
counselors steer us toward pharmacy school, and we end up counting
pills while looking longingly at the clouds. We've missed our calling.

Now, while Anne Frank's calling was to become a storyteller and use her pen, *your* calling may be to teach, help heal others, tend the earth and grow food, or just be the very best window washer you can. In this chapter, we're going to journey to the Chamber of Treasures to recover a tool that will allow you to express whatever your calling is—because a calling without a tool is like a race-car driver without a Ferrari. And frankly, there's nothing more frustrating than a person born with a great aptitude for music, poetry, or science who never develops it, and nothing more tiresome than someone who talks endlessly about how he wants to be an artist but refuses to obtain any skills to help him achieve that goal.

Medicine Gifts

Your newly recovered soul part will gather whatever implements it needs to express its mission and purpose. In fact, these tools are "medicine gifts" because they carry within them the power to manifest a new dimension of expression in your life—they'll enable you to board a new train to a fresh destination.

Coming in many shapes and forms, tools are metaphors, so yours may be a paintbrush or even something as simple as a stone or a grain of rice. These medicine gifts are never only what they seem to be: They have a mythical, mysterious quality that you must find for yourself. A pen that you discover in the Chamber of Treasures, for instance, isn't simply a writing instrument, it's also a tool that will call forth your inner poet.

However, you can't expect these tools to just be sitting and waiting for you, like a diamond ring in a jewelry store. What makes the ring precious in the first place is that the stone first had to be extracted from the earth at great human cost. We treasure gemstones for their beauty, but also because of what it takes to retrieve them—their value stems from the rare and extraordinary circumstance that they exist at all.

Like digging for diamonds, you have to journey deep into the Chamber of Treasures to find tools of value. They'll be the gifts of your subconscious, not the wrenches and pliers of your everyday work or family life. In other words, these aren't the pens you use to sign checks, but the quills used to write poetry. They're the materials of the mystic, sage, artist, and scientist.

Now, although we tend to look at things in the context of "bigger is better," in reality the simplest tool is often best: We buy enormous SUVs and forget how to use our legs until they're too weak to serve us; we shop for the perfect outdoor grill, while forgetting how to start a fire; we order the most expensive laptop computer to write a novel when a pen and paper will do; and we forget that myths and legends are filled with heroes and heroines overcoming incredible obstacles with basic tools that were just right for them.

David's Simple and Effective Tool

The biblical story of David and Goliath tells how a young shepherd changed the course of Western civilization with a mere slingshot.

The youngest of eight sons, David lived with his family in Bethlehem during the reign of King Saul. The young man tended his father's sheep, staying with them day and night to defend them against predators. He once slayed a lion that was stealing a sheep, and another time he killed a bear that was carrying away a lamb—in both instances, he used only his slingshot. And in the long evenings before the fire, he played his harp and made up songs about God that he sang as he watched over his sleeping flock.

Meanwhile, David's three older brothers were soldiers in the king's army, which was locked in a desperate battle against the Philistines, who had many giants in their ranks. The fiercest of them all was Goliath, who stood more than nine feet tall. For 40 days, this massive figure stalked the edge of the cliff where the Philistine armies were camping and called across the valley to King Saul. "Choose one man to come fight me!" he yelled. "If he can kill me, the Philistines will be your servants. If I kill him, you will become our slaves." Goliath struck fear into the hearts of King Saul's soldiers, and not one man stepped forth to fight him.

One day, David's father gathered bread, wheat, and cheese into a sack and told his son to take it to his brothers on the battlefront so that they would have something proper to eat. When David arrived at the camp, he heard Goliath bellowing across the valley to the terrified soldiers. They knew that their weapons wouldn't protect them; David, on the other hand, believed that God stood by him, so he went before King Saul and volunteered to go into combat against Goliath.

The king was skeptical of David's offer. All he saw standing before him was a small shepherd in a wool frock, untrained in the art of war. He told the young man that he doubted he'd stand a chance against the giant, and the risk to his kingdom was too great in the likely event that David failed.

David replied, "I used to keep my father's sheep, and when a lion came and took a lamb from the flock, I went after it and delivered the lamb from its mouth and killed the lion. The Lord who delivered me from the paw of the lion will deliver me from the hand of this Philistine."

King Saul could see that David wasn't like other men, so he offered the shepherd his coat of armor and helmet, the traditional tools of war. But the armor was too heavy for David, so he took it off and went on with just his slingshot. At a stream in the valley, he stopped and gathered five smooth stones and placed them in his pouch before climbing the hill to the Philistine camp. When Goliath saw David—without armor or a helmet and carrying only a slingshot—he cursed him and shouted, "Am I a dog that you come against me with sticks?!"

Breathing a quick prayer, David placed one of the smooth rocks in his slingshot and drew back the band. When he released it, the stone shot through the air, straight into the forehead of the giant, knocking him backward on the ground. David quickly ran and grasped the giant's sword from its sheath, and then he cut off Goliath's head. The Philistine soldiers were stunned and ran away in a panic. King Saul's army chased after them, and the people in the nearby towns shouted, danced, and sang for joy because of David's victory. Later, after King Saul's death, David became king of Israel.

Our Own Slingshot

The story of David and Goliath illustrates what can happen when we respond to our calling with the right tool, even when it's as simple as an ordinary slingshot. Even though everyone looked upon him as a lowly shepherd, David knew in his heart that he was a king. And in order to step into his destiny, he needed to use his own tools, not those of King Saul or any other soldier. No one else may have been able to slay Goliath with a slingshot, but David could because it was the right instrument for him. Similarly, if we journey deeply enough, we're certain to find what's right for us.

As with David, our tools have often been right in front of us for our entire lives, but we have to grow into seeing their value before we can actually use them. In the myth of Parsifal, what he needs to change his life and destiny is literally right under his nose in the form of his voice. All he has to do is recognize its innate power and learn to use it to ask the crucial question of the Grail. Instead, Parsifal matures into a strong, silent man of action who has no ability to voice his wonder at the world. He relies on his sword and armor because they're what his father wielded: the ordinary tools of knights. Yet opportunity after opportunity passes him by because he doesn't use his voice to speak for himself. He misses out on conjugal love because he doesn't ask Blanche Fleur, "Am I the one you've been waiting for?" He finds the Grail in his youth, but doesn't ask the question that will bring him into his destiny. Parsifal wastes these precious chances to step into his destiny by hiding within his armor, until he finally puts his voice to its proper use, and the power of the Grail is revealed to him.

Psyche also uses very simple tools to accomplish her four tasks: She makes use of the ants to sort the seeds, the reeds to gather the golden fleece, the eagle to capture the water from the river Styx, and the coins and barley cakes to get herself in and out of Hades. But like Parsifal, perhaps the most important tool Psyche uses is her newfound ability to say yes to her calling and no to the things that would distract her, such as the drowning man and the three women weaving the strands of fate. The ability to say no is crucial for you as well: The journey is about *you* right now, not about anybody else asking for your help.

The stories of Parsifal and Psyche show that the tools we're given carry mandates for their use, so we must be careful to employ them for the correct task. If Parsifal only uses his voice to talk to himself in the mirror, then it's worthless as a tool. If Psyche eats the barley cakes instead of feeding them to Cerberus, or uses the coins to go shopping, she'll fail in her quest to discover her inner beauty. If David hadn't used his slingshot, he would have remained a shepherd, King Saul's army would have been defeated, and the young man never would have become a king.

When we find our own voice or our own slingshot, it can set us on a course for destiny . . . but it doesn't mean that we no longer have to fight the giant. Our tool isn't a magic wand that makes everything better—it's something that allows us to confront situations that we find insurmountable, overwhelming, and dispiriting. As in the case of King Saul and his army, when our emotional resources are drained and our wealth of positive energy and inspiration become inaccessible, we're often deadlocked and unable to move forward. A tool as simple as a slingshot can allow us to change the course of the world—just like in David's story, the risk is enormous, the conditions are desperate, and the payoff is extraordinary. When we employ our deeply buried treasures to serve our calling, the results are nothing short of miraculous: We go from being shepherds to becoming kings in our inner lives.

Discovering a Creative Tool

The tool you find on your journey may change your life, making you realize your calling. When my client Sally entered the Chamber of Treasures, for example, she discovered a gold pen that told her that it came with a proviso that the first person to pick it up wouldn't be able to put it down. Sally hesitated, because she'd always dreamed of being a writer, but she'd never found the time to write. She not only had to run a household, but she also assisted her husband with the bookkeeping for his business and had a full-time practice as a healer.

Next to the pen, Sally also found an hourglass, and she brought both gifts back with her. In the following weeks, she held the hourglass, trying to determine its significance. When she discovered that she could turn it over and the sand would begin flowing the other way, she realized that she had the ability to make time, and that her time was her own. As a result, she began cutting back on the hours she spent working. She then used her gold pen, which began telling her about the stories she had within her. True to her journey, she hasn't been able to put the pen down since! Sally has completed her first book of stories and is currently working on a second one.

Creative tools can be instruments of salvation when used to their full potential. When the great Mexican painter Frida Kahlo was horribly injured in a bus accident, the only thing that gave her the strength to go on was tapping in to her artistic talent. She had one choice—create or die. Many of her paintings graphically illustrate the pain and suffering she went through, and their very existence testifies to her power. Another example of a simple yet transformational gift can be found in the 2002 film *The Pianist*. The movie follows the story of the amazing Polish pianist Wladyslaw Szpilman, who survived the harrowing Nazi occupation of Warsaw through his ability to play the piano. Music nourished his spirit and kept his soul alive in the face of absolute misery.

Moving from Imaginal to Practical

The intangible, inner tools that we find in the Chamber of Treasures are sometimes difficult to recognize and put to use. It takes contemplation to understand how to use an object as a tool, and to uncover its intended purpose in our lives. In one of my early visits to the Amazon, for instance, a shaman gave me an alabaster conch shell the size of my hand as a gift after my soul retrieval. It's a treasure I've now had for many years, but it took me months to truly understand what I was supposed to do with it.

At the time, the shaman told me, "Let it speak to you. Discover what its medicine is." So I carried the shell with me. I could appreciate how beautiful it was, and if I blew through the hole in the end, I could make a sound with it. I held it to my ear—I couldn't hear the ocean, but I discovered that it did amplify everything I heard. It was then that

I realized part of my lesson: I needed to learn to listen better to my calling. I discovered that *my* calling had to do with calling others. It was a great teaching that came to me from just holding a simple shell.

Years later, I realized that in many traditional societies, the sound made by a conch is a call to prayer, and that part of my calling is to help others find their own gifts as healers and modern shamans. After I understood that the shell was a tool for summoning, I also realized that it had been built by an animal as a house, and that this animal walked underwater with its house on its back. I realized that to a great degree this was exactly what I was doing at the time: I was walking around in the Andes with my own portable house, which was my tent. I was carrying a big pack on my back, just like a shell, filled with camping gear that provided me with a sense of safety and protection. I had to ask myself if I really needed such a big shell at 14,000 feet when I had to carry it on my back like this creature did.

I then began to make many analogies about the baggage that I was carrying, and what I needed in order to feel comfortable and safe in the world. The shell showed me how to travel lightly, holding everyone I love in my heart, which is my true home. This conch is still a great tool for me, because what makes a tool isn't the use it was first created for, but the use to which we actually put it.

After finding our tool, we must come up with a way to transform it from a symbol to a practical instrument. To assist in this process, I'll often give my client an object that represents what I find in the Chamber of Treasures, just as the shaman gave me the gift of the shell. In this way, I can bring the tool from the imaginal to the physical realm of ordinary reality. I like to make it something that they can actually work with, carry, transport, meditate on, hold, and utilize, because then it will have an impact on their daily life.

I may bring back a stone, or I'll have them find a bowl and tell them, "This bowl holds your medicine—what do you want to put in it? Experiment! Put some water and flowers in it, or try some candles! What about the empty bowl: How do you become an empty vessel for Spirit? How do you prepare the cup for the wine?" The physical practice of holding the tool will bring forth its messages.

Laura's Healing Knife

Laura was a university program director who found herself entan-gled in webs of political intrigue in her work. She came to me looking for a different approach to healing.

During our journey together, I found a golden knife lying on a table in her Chamber of Treasures. I brought the symbol back with me and blew it energetically—the traditional way to "gift" the essence of a soul part, tool, or power animal—into her third chakra. (I'll discuss power animals in detail in the next chapter.) Afterward, I asked her to find a ceremonial knife, and Laura did so, picking up a beautiful one with turquoise embedded in the handle. She carried it around with her for the next six months.

In her meditation, she used this knife to sever the cords of toxic relationships, work intrigues, and restrictions she placed on herself. I asked her to move the knife slowly and deliberately over her body to symbolically cut the energy strands that bound her. I wanted her to dis-entangle herself from the cords that tied her to her past and to relation-ships that were suffocating her. These meditations also taught her to "sharpen her edge" so that she could hone her powers of discernment to make better decisions. At the same time, it taught her that she had to be careful not to use her tools of discernment as weapons against others, and to be mindful of how she wielded her own power.

I'd also brought back a spider as a power animal for Laura, which I'd blown into her second chakra, but neither Laura nor I understood the significance of this creature. What I didn't know at the time is that Laura was suffering from a severe lung disease called *sarcoidosis* and was not responding to treatment. Her doctor had advised her that a lung transplant was a distinct possibility, which frightened her not only because of the complexity of the operation, but also because she was the single parent of seven-year-old twin girls.

Laura had been bitten on the left hand by a poisonous spider a few years earlier. Her hand had swollen up and the bite had filled with pus, but after it healed she never gave it another thought. Although she hadn't previously made the connection, she now realized that it was after the bite that her lung disease appeared and she became seriously ill.

After meditating on her power animal, Laura grasped the relationship between the spider bite and the "webs" in which she was caught. As soon as she began to cut herself free from all the entanglements in her life, her system was able to clear the poison that caused her illness. Later, her power animal taught her that *everything* gets trapped in the spiderweb—except the spider itself.

Laura's lung function returned to normal and she was able to travel with me to Peru on one of our annual expeditions, even camping at 14,000 feet with no problems. Her physical healing spurred great emotional and spiritual growth as well.

What's _Your_ Tool?

Now it's time to journey to the final chamber of the Lower World— that of treasures—where you'll find your own tool, that mythical "slingshot" that will conquer the twin behemoths of apathy and resistance to change. You'll ask for a deeply buried instrument to bring back with you, something you can put to use in your daily life. It may turn out to be a creative tool, like Sally's pen; it may be a healing tool, like Laura's knife; or it may be a tool that helps you grow or find your purpose—but remember, just as gemstones are hidden far below the surface and require considerable effort to extract, harvesting these deeply buried treasures won't come easily. You'll have to be steadfast, even if someone else doesn't see this gift within you, or says: "You're a writer? You've got to be kidding. You're a mom!" And then you'll have to refine it, as a craftsperson makes jewelry, to turn it into a thing of beauty.

When you find your tool, you'll carry it back from the Lower World of potential and possibility and into the physical world of action and expression. Just as David challenged and defeated Goliath with his slingshot, Psyche used her coins and barley cakes to travel safely in and out of Hades, and Parsifal used his voice, your own tool is sacred medicine that will propel you toward the creative expression of your particular gifts.

Prepare for this journey by creating the proper intention: Be open to receiving the gift that this tool represents, as well as the challenges and demands it brings with it.

Exercise: Journey to the Chamber of Treasures

Open sacred space, perform the little-death exercise, and journey to your garden in the Lower World.

State your intent to find your sacred tool, and ask the gatekeeper to guide you into the Chamber of Treasures. When you enter, ask for an instrument that you can use to express your gifts. As before, engage in a dialogue with the figure you find there, whether it be a person, a table, or a goblet, and ask questions to determine the nature of your tool and how it can be used. When I journey to this chamber, I like to think of it as having many props, including bookshelves, chests, a fireplace, and a table in the center. I know that the tool my client needs will be on the table. But sometimes the table is empty, and I must part the cobwebs on the shelf or open a trunk to discover an instrument that's been hidden from view.

Search around the room (you can also ask the gatekeeper for guidance and advice). When you find your tool, take it. What is it to be used for? What can it teach you?

When you've retrieved your medicine object, begin your journey out, thank the gatekeeper, dive into the waters, and return to the room and into your body bearing your tool. Hold it in the palm of your hand and bring it into whichever chakra you're guided to. If you get no specific instructions, bring it into your heart chakra. Remember that this is an energetic gift— inhale deeply and feel its energy and power filling every cell in your body.

Close your sacred space.

Exercise: Finding the Object at Home

Search for an object in your home that closely resembles the tool you've uncovered. *Do not go out and purchase one!* Remember that our tools are most often right under our noses. Search through your closets and drawers until you find the one thing that most closely approximates the instrument that you received. Sit with this object in meditation, turn it over in your hands, and let it instruct and guide you toward the gifts it wants to express.

Exercise: Journal Dialogue with the Tool

After you've retrieved your tool from the Lower World, this journal exercise will help you learn more about its role in your life.

Begin by opening sacred space. Then take your journal and draw a line down the center of a blank page. On the left side, write questions for your tool; on the right side, write down the answers it provides. Your questions might include: "How can I best use you?" "How can I bring you into my everyday life?" "How can I make you practical?" "What outdated tools do I need to let go of in order to work with you?" "Are there tools I no longer need?" "How will you bring forth my creativity?" and "How do you serve as an instrument of healing for me?"

Allow the dialogue to flow—don't rush.

Close sacred space when you're finished.

In the next chapter, you'll learn about retrieving your power animal, which will teach you to heed your natural instincts.

CHAPTER EIGHT

The Power Animals

I am moving. And breathing.

I move through a many-layered collage of wet leaves, hanging vines, reds, yellows, and greens washed gray by moonlight. My head hangs low to the ground. Faster, I pant. The ground yields slightly beneath the pads of my . . . hands and feet? They move in cadence with the throbbing in my chest. My breath is hot and humid, my heart beats too fast, and I can smell myself beyond the moist tangle of the jungle.

There is the clearing and there am I, sitting cross-legged, naked, and shining wet in the moonlight. My head is thrown back and my throat is taut, exposed. Arms thrown out lax to my sides, hands palm up on the soil.

I watch myself from the edge of the jungle. Still, but for my breathing. Behind me, the jungle stirs sleeplessly.

I move with the lithesomeness of a shadow, following the contours of the clearing's edge to circle my prey.

Soundlessly. Closer.

Now we are breathing together. My head falls forward. My chin touches my chest. I raise my head, open my eyes to stare into yellow cat eyes, my eyes, animal eyes. A half-breath catches in my throat, and I reach out to the face of the jungle cat.

— from Alberto's journal[1]

If you talk to the animals, they will talk with you, and you will know each other. If you do not talk to them, you will not know them, and what you do not know, you will fear. What one fears, one destroys.
— from *Animal-Speak,* by Ted Andrews[2]

Dolphins appeal to us because they appear to be so playful and free. We feel a sense of connectedness to them, and they in turn seem to greet us from the sea like nature's ambassadors—intelligent, sleek, and acrobatic, swimming alongside our boats and calling to us with squeaks and clicks. The ancient Greeks thought of dolphins as sacred messengers, and blessed them as symbols of the sea. Dolphins can teach us many things, including how to loosen up, enjoy life, and breathe deeply . . . but they're just one of the many animals from which we can learn.

Even the smallest, most ordinary of creatures can be wise instructors. For example, we like to think of mice and other rodents as pests, but as with all animals, we need to consider the *entire* "nature of the beast." Small and plentiful, mice are survivors—they can squeeze into small places and travel underground, they store food, and they have three or four litters a year to increase their odds of enduring as a species. Also, mice are seen by some African cultures as the couriers of messages to the underworld, making them a powerful connection to one's ancestors.

In fact, from the earliest times, humankind has expressed its reverence for the natural world by using animals as totems and symbols of the highest ideals: The earth's fauna have been used to express the strength of rulers (the lion), the purity of God (the lamb), and the sacred principles of the universe (the serpent and the eagle). The Toltecs and other Meso-American societies worshiped the winged serpent Quetzalcoatl, a god who was master of the winds and the sky, and the protector of his people. In Greek mythology, Medusa's scalp writhed with live snakes, symbolic of her sovereign female wisdom (but one glance at her was said to turn a man to stone), while the hero Hercules was often shown wearing a lion skin, which gave him the beast's cunning, strength, and dominance over the animal world.

The stories of the Bible are filled with animal references as well: King Solomon is referred to as the "lion of Judea," and Jesus is called the "lamb of God." In the Hindu religion, cows are held to be sacred; and there are animal gods such as Hanuman, the monkey god; and Ganesh, the elephant god. The zodiac also has many animals as its symbols, as does the Chinese calendar.

Cultural identifications with animals are so strong that entire civilizations have taken them as their symbols. For example, the mighty lion, symbol of courage, has long represented England; and the industrious honeybee, a symbol of immortality and resurrection, was chosen as an emblem by both Charlemagne and Napoleon to represent France.

Perhaps the most omnipresent animal symbol of all has been the eagle, which has been adopted by both ancient and modern cultures around the world. This magnificent bird has been associated with the Greeks, Egyptians, Sumerians, Hittites, and Romans, all of whom used it as an emblem for their formidable empires. The bald eagle was also chosen to represent the might and freedom of the United States.

The Animal Archetype in the Western World

While in our Western culture we behave as though all of nature is ours to subjugate at our will—after all, in the first book of the Bible, humans *were* given every creature on the planet—most indigenous cultures still live in harmony with animals. As with all Native American peoples, the Laika understand themselves to be the caretakers of all life, and they strive to live in harmony with nature and to communicate directly with it. Indigenous Americans have many traditional animal dances (such as those of the snake, eagle, and deer), in which participants wear the skins of the animals to embody their spirits so that they'll be able to move more easily in their world during the hunt or through journeying. By summoning the spirit of that animal, they embody its essence, often wearing their fur or feathers to be empowered by its attributes.

When an Osage Indian dancer put on a buffalo headdress, it was to ask permission to take the life of a buffalo, in the hopes that the animal would be renewed with life the following year. The Osage didn't seek to exterminate the buffalo—they honored it and respected its awesome powers. They understood that they could just as easily be trampled to death by these magnificent beasts as they could succeed in taking one during the hunt.

By living with respect for nature, becoming part of its cyclical character, and understanding their place in it, the Osage only took what they needed for food, and in turn, their resources were renewed over and over again. Nothing could have been in greater contrast to this than the arrival of the white man in the American West in the 18th and 19th centuries: They shot buffalo for profit and sport and slaughtered millions of animals, bringing about the demise of the great herds and hastening the end of the natural lifestyle of many indigenous tribes.

These days, in our commercially oriented culture, animal imagery is often used in advertising or as a business logo because we intuitively respond to the meaning of each animal's attributes. We know what the jaguar means when it comes to a sports car—it will be sleek, fast, and elite, just as the animal is one of the swiftest and most revered of the jungle. Dodge's best-selling truck is called the Ram because, like that animal, it's sure-footed on rocky terrain.

But apart from archetypal images used in advertising, most of us have lost our sense of connectedness to all but the most domesticated of animals. Our only contact with wild animals is through watching them on television or observing them in locked cages at the zoo. So, in this chapter, we'll journey to the Lower World to retrieve a power that represents the instinctual aspects of the soul in its natural, most unspoiled state.

The Four Spirit Animals of the Laika

Like many Native Americans, the Laika are so closely linked to the animal world that they often take an animal as their namesake. By doing so, they're seeking to be associated with the animal's energies and to embody its powers. Four archetypal animals are particularly important to the Laika: the serpent, the jaguar, the eagle (or condor), and the hummingbird. (You may remember that we invoke these four spirit animals, representing the four core principles of life, in our prayer to create sacred space.)

Let's look at each archetype in depth.

1. The Serpent

The serpent symbolizes knowledge, sexuality, and the healing power of nature. It is a universal archetype: When Moses led the Israelites through the desert, he carried a serpent staff that symbolized wisdom; a serpent in the Garden of Eden tempted Eve to eat the forbidden fruit from the Tree of Knowledge; in the East, the snake symbolizes the sage Kundalini energy that lies coiled at the base of the spine and channels up through the chakras; and the physicians' symbol, *caduceus,* which dates from ancient Greece, depicts two serpents intertwined around a staff. Associated with wisdom and healing, the serpent represents the essential life force that seeks union and creation.

Serpents are also symbols of fertility. In nature, fecundity is the creative principle associated with the feminine—after all, every cell in the body seeks to divide and procreate. When we engage the energies of the serpent archetype, we summon the feminine creative principle that can rekindle our passion and help us shed the past, as a snake sheds its skin.

2. The Jaguar

The jaguar is the king of the Amazon rain forest, and the most important animal for the jungle shaman because it represents the power of transformation. It's of such primary importance that anthropologist Peter Furst writes: "Shamans and jaguars are not merely equivalent, but each is the same as each other." This should come as no surprise: In the lore of the rain-forest peoples, jaguars are seen as the caretakers of the jungle because they're at the top of the food chain and have no predators other than man.

By weeding out the weaker animals of the forest, the jaguar helps eliminate that which must die in order for the new to be born. Thus, this creature teaches us that crisis becomes a time of opportunity, and death is a call to rebirth. In the jungle, survival entails constant renewal—and the jaguar is a force of change, of life and death. The Laika understand that stable, steady states are only temporary, because everything in the universe is always dying and being reborn. They recognize that chaos and order (or expansion and contraction) represent the natural cycle of life.

Jaguar energy can renew an individual, an organization, or a village. Sometimes, in response to the cyclical nature of order and chaos, a village must be abandoned so that its members can thrive in a different location—in fact, throughout the Americas, archaeological evidence shows that Mayan and Inkan settlements were deserted for no apparent reason. The abandonment of these cities is a reflection of the life-death cycle represented by the jaguar.

Jaguars held such power for ancient peoples that entire civilizations identified with them. The Olmecs, who thrived 3,000 years ago in central Mexico, were the first advanced civilization of the Americas. Known as the "jaguar people" (and their shamans were the "jaguar priests"), nearly half of their carvings and statuary are anthropomorphic representations of humans and felines; many are adults and children with jaguar heads. And the Mayoruna, an indigenous tribe in the Amazon rain forest, call themselves "people of the jaguar": They tattoo their faces to look like cats, and even insert boar whiskers into piercings on the sides of their noses to resemble the large felines.

In his book *Amazon Beaming*, Petru Popescu tells the story of the *National Geographic* photographer and explorer Loren McIntyre (famous for discovering the source of the Amazon in the Peruvian Andes in 1971), who lived among the Mayoruna for many months in the 1960s. McIntyre reported that aside from their native tongue, the Mayoruna seemed to have developed the ability to communicate their thoughts telepathically, beaming unspoken messages into their fellow tribesmen's heads.

The ability to communicate without words is one of the legendary attributes of the jaguar shamans. In my early travels to the Amazon, my mentor, an old Laika, asked me to spend the night in a jungle clearing on a vision quest. He was going to be calling on the jaguars to come and visit me, and cautioned me not to fall asleep.

Before the vision quest, just as the sun was setting, he invited me to drink ayahuasca, the mind-altering brew of the jungle. I politely declined the glass of the foul-tasting liquid—I'd already had enough fear and trepidation about spending the night alone in the jungle in my ordinary state of consciousness. Nothing out of the ordinary happened until I dozed off; when I awoke, I was no longer myself—suddenly, I was in the body of a large cat! To embody the jaguar was an unforgettable experience.

3. The Eagle

The eagle is a powerful spirit animal that symbolizes foresight, clarity, and vision. The shaman understands that eagle energy helps us perceive the entire panorama of life without becoming bogged down in its myriad tiny details. Eagle energy can assist us in finding the guiding vision of our lives by looking into the past *and* the future, helping us understand both where we came from and who we're becoming.

The eagle gives us wings to soar up to the high peaks, far above our trivial day-to-day struggles. It has tremendous vision—with six times the visual acuity of humans, this incredible bird can spot a mouse in a clump of brush from 1,500 feet up in the air. It can see the big picture and swoop down and take what it needs with unhesitating precision.

The eagle also represents the self-transcending principle of nature (as such, it's often associated with the Upper World instead of the Lower World). Biologists have identified this principle as one of the prime agendas of nature. It guides the hand of evolution—that is, living molecules unite to become cells, which form tissues, then organs, and finally transcend a collection of organs and tissues to become complex beings such as whales and humans. Each transcending jump is inclusive of all the levels beneath it: Cells are inclusive of molecules, yet transcend them; organs are inclusive of cells yet go far beyond them; and scarlet macaws are inclusive of organs yet cannot be described by them, as the whole transcends the sum of its parts. The problems of cells are best resolved by organs, while the needs of organs are best addressed by an organism such as a butterfly or a human that can secure food and safety more effectively.

The same principle operates in our daily lives. The eagle shows us that we can't satisfy our emotional needs with material things, and that there's a spiritual solution to every problem. On the wings of the eagle, we rise above our day-to-day struggles, gain perspective, and see things as they really are.

4. The Hummingbird

Tiny, feisty, and courageous, the hummingbird shows us how to embark on an epic journey of evolution and growth. This is the most noble journey a person can undertake: the journey to one's spirit. Every year, a certain species of hummingbird takes an incredible voyage, migrating from Brazil to Canada across the Caribbean Sea. At first glance, these little creatures wouldn't seem suited for such a long flight—they don't have a broad wingspan as eagles do, and their little bodies can't store much food—still, they respond to an annual call to undertake this incredible journey.

When we're touched by the energies of this archetype, we're propelled on our own epic journey that leads us back to our source, where our spirit was spawned. When we don't have enough time, money, or knowledge for what we're attempting, hummingbird energy can provide the courage, strength, and guidance that we need to succeed.

When we deny our calling, we begin to die, because as living beings we must always seek to explore and discover. When we settle for comfort over discovery—or when we compromise the soul's longing to grow, postponing our adventurous journey until we have enough time or money—we begin to wither. But when we follow the example of the hummingbird and reawaken our natural instinct to learn and explore, our lives blossom into epic quests.

What the Wolf Taught Me

The beauty of soul retrieval is that Spirit will provide you with whatever power animal you need without your having to figure it out, because it isn't a rational process. You simply have to work with what's given to you and explore the animal's attributes as it reveals its wisdom. You'll call on a power animal, and it'll leap out and follow you back . . . then it's up to you to discover how you're going to work with it.

For example, when my son was born, I retrieved the wolf as a power animal. He came to me unexpectedly and clung closely to my side. He informed me that he was going to teach me how to be deeply loyal to my family, as he was to his pack, yet be able to roam widely. He told me that his qualities were commitment and dedication without compromising individuality, which were the lessons I needed to learn, since I'd spent much of my adult life as an explorer in the Andes and the Amazon. The wolf taught me loyalty and independence. It taught me to be part of a family pack without feeling constrained by it. I learned that I could best serve my family by retaining my identity and sense of purpose in life at the same time.

Now, even though power animals symbolize the attributes we need to acquire to become whole, they also have pitfalls. The female jaguar, for instance, is fiercely dedicated to her young and amazingly protective, but the male jaguar is only around her for two weeks of the year—the rest of the time he's marking territory a few dozen miles away. So, if you've become too homebound and domesticated, or if you want to come back to your explorer self, you might work with the male jaguar energy; yet if you lack a protective parent, or if you want to increase your sense of safety in the world, you might need the female jaguar. Just be sure to keep the strengths *and* weaknesses of your power animal in mind as you work with it.

Patty's Ox

A few months after her wedding, a young client of mine named Patty retrieved an ox as a power animal. She was a writer who worked in a home office with her new husband, and here's her account of what happened:

> I was really excited about my marriage, but I also felt burdened by the change it had brought about in my life. I didn't feel comfortable with the day-to-day negotiations about chores and money; I was uncertain about what it meant to be married, how much my new husband would take care of me, and how much independence I could retain; and I didn't know how to be nurturing with my husband and at the same time be free from the expectations of being "Patty Homemaker." Yet, rather than discussing these issues with my husband, I just tried to do everything myself, which led to feelings of resentment and exhaustion.
>
> When I first brought back my power animal, I was puzzled by the big lumbering creature that came to me—but when I engaged the ox in dialogue, it informed me that he was my partner. He said that he was there to work with me and share my load. He was accustomed to being yoked to another ox, pulling as a team for their entire lives. When the two animals are nurtured, they work together, each pulling far more than its own weight, but also only carrying half the burden. When the partnership works, there's almost nothing a pair of oxen can't do together.
>
> He told me that because the ox is so powerful, it's easy to overlook its vulnerabilities. We all know the expression "as strong as an ox," but this animal can be killed through overwork—just as you can kill a relationship when one partner is working to please the other at the expense of his or her own needs and desires. And an ox can be very inflexible, refusing to work with a partner it doesn't like or to change its ways. The danger is in being "as stubborn as an ox" and refusing to cooperate or resolve differences. And there's nothing like an ox that just wants to pull its own way—particularly when it's yoked to another animal!

The ox had a lot to teach Patty about developing nurturing partnerships, long-term commitment, and equality. She needed to learn to step in stride with her husband, each one carrying an equal load. As a beast of burden, the ox needs to be watered, cared for, and rested—similarly, Patty needed to learn to communicate her needs so that she wouldn't feel overworked and resentful later. She needed to pull her *own* weight, without subconsciously expecting her partner to work as her beast of burden.

Patty began to see the opportunities in the ox as a power animal and what it taught her about collaboration, steadfastness, and hard work, but she also realized how to harness its earthy, plodding energy. She needed to learn how to gently guide her new life in order to yield its greatest potential. The needs of the ox are basic, fundamental, and essential.

Using Your Animal Instincts

Retrieving a power animal is the final element in your journey to the Lower World. At the end of the journey, you'll call out for a power animal to accompany you back. Quite often, this will be one you haven't foreseen, perhaps something as simple as a caterpillar or a swallow, or as rare as a crocodile. Whatever the animal is, embrace it, bring it with you, and integrate its gifts. Learn how to move through the world with its energy.

Sometimes you'll retrieve a power animal that you dislike, perhaps a serpent. Remember that it represents an instinctual part of yourself that you may have become disconnected from, and even find distasteful. Many people don't like serpents, but a snake power animal can teach you to move sinuously through life and to feel your environment with your entire being. You must accept the power animal that comes to you, unless it's an insect. (Since insects are associated with the Lower World, it is best not to bring them out of their natural spiritual habitat.) *Working with a power animal is an instinctual process about who you're becoming, not about who you'd prefer to be in your own mind.*

Retrieving a power animal will connect you to your natural, unspoiled state—without these resources, it's easy to overintellectualize the journeying process. Your animal will ground you in your instinctual self, and you can embody its teachings by communicating with it and learning its rhythms, movements, and way of perceiving the world. For example, if you should discover a lynx as your power animal, you might wake up in the morning and stretch your limbs like a cat, find the grace of the feline's walk, imagine life through its eyes, and feel the world through its senses.

Physical exercises can also help you embody the essence of your power animal. For example, when you shake hands with someone, you'll do so in the dynamic way that a jaguar might do it, conveying power and stillness with your touch; or you'll look at the world the way a mouse would, one small chunk at a time. By embodying your power animal, you'll learn how to rely more on your instincts to guide you than your rational mind. (Your animal's instincts will also protect the soul part that has come home to you.)

Exercise: Journey to Retrieve your Power Animal

Prepare for this journey by opening sacred space. Sit comfortably, fix your gaze in front of you (or close your eyes), and take your hands into prayer pose at your heart. Voice your intention to get in touch with your power animal on this journey. Open sacred space. Perform the little-death exercise, and journey to your garden in the Lower World. When you greet the gatekeeper, state your intent to meet your power animal.

Sit on a stone in the meadow in your garden, and sense the spirit animal approaching you from behind. Feel how the hair on the back of your neck begins to stand on end, and sense how the animal's eyes are resting on you as it draws closer. Listen to its breathing behind you. Now turn around, and in your imagination open your eyes, and look into those of your power animal. Reach out with your hand and touch its beak, fur, antlers, scales, or fins.

Gaze into its eyes, and ask: "What gifts do you bring to me?" "What is your medicine?" "What are your attributes?" "What are your strengths?" "What are your weaknesses?" "How will you assist me in my healing?" "How long have you been tracking me?" "How can I care for and feed you?" and "Why you and not another power animal?" Engage in this dialogue for as long as you need to.

When you're ready, invite your power animal to come back with you. Take your leave from the gatekeeper, the Lord of Life and Death. Dive into the waters, calling on your spirit animal to return with you. Take a big stretch, rub your hands together, rub your face, and open your eyes. (Come back into the room and into your body.)

Next, reach out with your hands and feel the energy of your power animal, and then bring it toward you. Take it into which- ever chakra it guides you to. Sense its energy infusing every cell in your body. Begin to move your shoulders, your hands, and your head like that animal might move. Sense how it merges into your body. Close sacred space.

Exercise: A Journal Dialogue with Your Power Animal

This exercise will lead you to find the unique gifts of your power animal and discover its voice. Remember, this creature often symbol- izes a neglected or shadow part of the self. It can represent parts of yourself that you're not comfortable with, and it isn't uncommon for someone who dislikes reptiles to receive a cobra or a rattlesnake for a spirit animal.

Once you begin your dialogue with your power animal, you'll notice that this animal may begin appearing to you in dreams or meditations. This exercise will allow you to discover its secrets.

As before, start by opening sacred space and then drawing a line down the center of a blank journal page. On one side, you'll be asking questions; on the other, the voice of your power animal will answer. Begin by asking simple questions, but allow enough time for a full dialogue to emerge.

The following is an example of Patty's dialogue with her power animal:

Patty: Who are you?
Ox: I'm your partner. I'm here to share your load. We have to share our stride, since we'll be yoked together. You

can't get ahead of me, and I can't get ahead of you. Every day, we'll be strapped into the yoke and will move together; and we'll stay together, moving in harmony, for many years to come.

Patty: What will we do together?

Ox: We will work. We're beasts of burden, but we provide the sustenance of life. We till the soil, we turn millstones, we make sugar from cane. Together, step by step, we do great work.

Patty: How do I take care of you?

Ox: Treat me as your equal—feed me properly and give me water and rest. We'll always be together, every day. Step by step, we will get the job done.

Patty: Why have you come to me?

Ox: Because you need help. You can't finish all your projects alone. You do better with someone by your side to pick you up when your energy flags. You need a partner to walk in stride with you. I am that partner.

Close sacred space when you're finished.

Exercise: Embodying Your Power Animal

Now that you've explored your power animal, you'll learn to embody some of its qualities. This should be a conscious practice during the day. You might get up and stretch the way your animal stretches in the morning, or reach for a cup of coffee (or tea) the way *it* reaches for things. Or you might scan the scene in front of you with the vision of an eagle, taking it all in.

Use the senses of the animal, become the power animal, cohabitate with it, and share its identity so that you no longer *have* a power animal—you *are* that power animal.

In the next section, we'll begin our journey for destiny, but before we do, it might be useful to review the lessons learned in the soul-retrieval journey. Go back over your journal exercises from Part II and reread them. Take your time, and absorb their teachings.

Part III

the UPPER WORLD

CHAPTER NINE

Navigating Destiny:
Love, Power,
Money, and Health

*By the age of 30, I had experienced several significant
relationships. Then one morning I woke up and discovered I
had experienced only one relationship over and over. . . .
If you don't learn it, you end up marrying it.*
— from Alberto's journal

The Austrian psychiatrist Viktor Frankl developed the ideas for his best-selling book, *Man's Search for Meaning,* over the three years he spent imprisoned in Nazi concentration camps during World War II. While living the nightmare of his confinement, he grew to understand that humans' deepest longing is to discover the meaning and purpose of life—how else, he wondered, could one survive such horrors? "Everything can be taken from a man," Frankl wrote, "but one thing: the last of the human freedoms—to choose one's attitude in any given set of circumstances, to choose one's own way."[1]

While many who survived the camps suffered post-traumatic stress and their lives were emotionally broken, Frankl went on to become a doctor, philosopher, and author of 32 books. He was awarded 29 honorary degrees before his death in 1997, as well as the Albert Schweitzer Medal. How did he accomplish all of this? Was he born with the seeds of greatness, or was he just an ordinary man who found an extraordinary destiny by responding to his calling?

Our oldest myths claim that we all enter the world with a calling in our souls. Carl Jung believed that when we don't heed our calling—and this is not a call to greatness, but a call to meaning—then a life is wasted. Frankl's greatness was his ability to articulate the human need to find meaning in existence, a need that transcends the external conditions of life. When Frankl stood in his destiny, fate couldn't defeat him, no matter how dire the circumstances. Likewise, when *we* say yes to our destiny, we're then able to transcend suffering and triumph over seemingly impossible odds.

To have significance, our destiny doesn't have to be grand or validated by public acclaim, as Frankl's was, but it must be imbued with meaning and purpose. This is entirely independent of whether we acquire material possessions, marry, raise a family, or become famous. We might find happiness with empty pockets and solitude, and we may also find pain and suffering with every comfort and beautiful companion in the world.

Destiny and the Future

Our destiny is not the same as our future: While the future is what will happen later, destiny is in every instant, and we can always make ourselves available to it. Destiny is saying yes to the calling we're born with, while fate is what happens when we fight or ignore our calling. This is a very ancient idea that runs counter to modern psychology and biology, which define our destiny by our psychological and genetic profiles. However, the more we identify ourselves by what our parents did or failed to do, what's been programmed in our chromosomes, or what we own or wear, then the more our story belongs to our ancestors and to others. We dull our lives by explaining them away with a list of causes that lie beyond our control.

Of course, everybody will have a future—after all, it's the function of the march of time—but only certain people will have a destiny, because they'll use the sacred tools available for creating it. Plato thought that since our fate and lot in life are already cast before we're born, they can only be changed by the intervention of the gods. But

I believe that fate can be turned into destiny when we discover the hidden meaning of our lives . . . which we can do by journeying.

We each choose a character and a calling before we're born—these are innate to our very being and can't be explained by psychological theories. We sometimes recognize these qualities in our children more easily than we do in ourselves: We wonder where their stubbornness, determination, or absentmindedness came from. Certainly, we applaud exceptional athletic skills or musical talent, but we fear other extraordinary characteristics such as a high need for movement and novelty that makes it difficult to sit still in class.

In today's medication-prone society, many of these children wind up getting treated with Ritalin, Prozac, and other drugs that would have numbed the creativity out of many of the geniuses of the past. We have to wonder: Are all of these really medical disorders, or could many be expressions of a unique calling? For instance, ADHD (attention deficit/hyperactivity disorder) could be useful if you live in the desert or the jungle and have to multitask—that is, you could listen for the lions while you cook and look after the children.

When we live in the future, looking forward to a day when we hope things will be better, we're bound to time, which creeps forward "in this petty pace from day to day," as Shakespeare said. But living in the future is really no different from living in the past: In both, we're in the grip of fate, constantly reliving the pain that we've experienced, or longing for something or someone different from what we currently have. We continually experience and reexperience our past stories without changing their outcomes.

We can break this cycle during the soul-retrieval process and heal our past, but that doesn't make our destiny. We can be free of the hand of fate and still be far removed from our life's calling, or we can be out of a bad relationship but not be with our life partner yet. In other words, healing our past simply means that we're no longer reliving old hurts.

Now, healing old hurts is no small thing: If we continue to carry them with us, we end up coloring our tomorrows with their pain and fear. In psychology, this mechanism is known as *projection,* and it's one of the hazards of the therapeutic process. A psychologist who's working from a wounded place can project his own problems onto a patient. For example, a therapist who was going through a very painful conflict with a sibling over an inheritance once told me, "Alberto, all of my clients are fighting over money." This sounded strange to me, because my own clients have a wide variety of problems. It was clear that this man was unconsciously attracting patients who were going through his own dilemma, and he was projecting his shadow onto them in an attempt to heal himself.

In a similar way, we project our unhealed hurts onto others—this is especially true when we journey for destiny in an unhealed state. We reinfect ourselves and our destinies by projecting our wounds onto our future, rather than experiencing life as an unfolding series of new experiences. If we don't heal, we'll spend our lives continually reinventing new versions of the same spouse, job, and opportunity—we'll whittle 20 years of experience into one year of experience repeated 20 times.

We simply cannot leap forward without healing our foundation. For example, when you started reading this book, it would have been appealing to just flip to the end and say, "I don't really want to explore my past. What's done is done. Let's forget about soul retrieval, and just get on with the business of destiny." But the soul-retrieval journey is an essential preparation, for it transplants the acorn of our potential from rocky ground to fertile earth. When we track destiny, we germinate the acorn of the great tree within us. We heal the past in order to journey to the Upper World, free of the traumas that have kept us from achieving our potential, and without the danger of infecting our future.

No Tracks, No Shadow, No Ego

The Laika tell us, "When we can walk on the snow and leave no tracks, when we cast no shadow, we don't disturb the ripples of time." Walking on the snow without leaving tracks means that we tread so lightly that we leave no trace of our passing, while to cast no shadow means that we don't project our wounded selves onto others—we don't like or dislike someone because they remind us of our mother or lover. We shine like a sun that casts no shadows.

This is how we must journey for destiny, because if we disturb the ripples of time, there will be an immediate backlash. The Greeks would have said that we "anger the fates," while the Hindus would say that we "fall into karma." So when we journey for destiny, we can't leave any tracks or interject our will. In order to tread lightly, we must dissolve the self, freeing ourselves from the whims of ego. We must let go of our "I" and become one with Spirit.

Once my Inka mentor and I were walking in the Altiplano, a high arid region in the Andes. We came to a village where it hadn't rained in many months, and the water supply was drying out. Because this man was a renowned Laika, the villagers implored him to call the rain. He went into a hut where he prayed, fasted, and meditated for four days. When he came out, I asked him, "What are you going to do?" And he said, "I am going to pray rain."

Not understanding, and thinking we were having a language problem, I asked him, "You mean you're going to pray *for* rain?"

"No," he replied. "I am going to *pray* rain."

He walked to the edge of the mountain, where a cliff wall dropped 3,000 feet to a white-water river below, and began to meditate. When he returned four hours later, there were big thunderheads in the sky—when they broke, the rains came.

Everybody in the village was ecstatic, for the rain was their salvation. They came running to him, and cried, "Thank you! You called the rain!" And he said, "No, *it rained.*"

I finally understood what the old man meant: He'd taken himself out of the equation. He'd prayed, and it rained, but he hadn't prayed *for* rain. There was no one to whom to pray to make it rain; there was no "other." He had become one with Spirit. There was only Spirit praying, and it rained.

This is what we do: We pray healing, and when healing happens, we're as surprised as the next person, because the will of Spirit has been at play, not our own. When we take ourselves out of the equation, when we're no longer "doing" anything or willing an outcome, we're only enacting Spirit. And it is in this egoless state that we can track our own destinies.

We have to let go of our ego, which is attached to a particular outcome. We can't have our hearts set on whether it rains or not, whether something is healed or not, or whether anything will be different from the way it is right now. We simply have to be one with Spirit and let it rain. Once we accept the world exactly as it is, we can influence the future by tracking along our time lines.

Time Lines

A time line is an imaginal cord of light reaching from the present into the past and future. All the events of our history are recorded in our time lines from past to present, because every action leaves a track in time. Our time lines also extend forward into the future as thousands of luminous strands, like fiber-optic threads that fan out of the cord of light, with each strand representing a possible future. You can track forward along your possible futures to discover your healed destiny, where your heart disease or breast cancer has been cured, your diet has changed, and your toxic relationships have been cleaned up.

Tracking along time lines has been put into practical use for millennia. In aboriginal societies, the shaman needs to lead her tribe to where the fish and game are going to be the following morning. She does this by tracking along the time line of the village, to find where the hunters need to wait for the prey at daybreak. So when we journey for destiny, we track not only for the probable, but also for the possible, no matter how *im*probable. If we only track for probable destinies, we'll never find the bison or the fish, a future healed state, or world peace. Instead, we'll reinforce negative probable futures, because the negative outcomes we find become installed into our time lines.

Once a student of mine journeyed into the Upper World, and all she saw along her destiny lines were illness and death (her family had a long history of heart disease). A few months later she became ill, because she'd only tracked along her probable destinies, not her *possible* destinies, which may have yielded an outcome free of disease.

In quantum physics, there's a theory called the "Heisenberg uncertainty principle," which says that the observer influences the outcome of events. Observe a subatomic particle, thinking it's a wave, and it will actually become a wave; expect to see a subatomic particle in a certain location, and it will be there. We can apply this principle to our own lives by understanding that whatever destiny we track will come to pass; after all, as seers know, *all* prophecies are self-fulfilling.

The film *Touching the Void* tells the true story of a pair of English climbers who are scaling a very dangerous and remote mountain in the Andes when a blinding snowstorm strikes. On the way down, one of them falls into a deep crevasse and breaks his leg. The other man has to make a difficult choice—cut the rope between them and save his own life, or stay tied to his partner and risk dying as well. He cuts the rope and makes it back to safety, thinking that he's lost his partner. Unbelievably, his left-for-dead partner is able to climb out of the crevasse and crawl back to camp. It takes him six days, but he makes it, and his friend is there waiting for him. Survival was scrawled in this man's destiny line, and he crawled toward it.

Putting the cart before the horse and looking at possibilities before looking at probabilities is essential when tracking destiny. In a televised broadcast in 1961, for example, President John F. Kennedy announced that by the end of the decade, America would land a man on the moon and return him safely to Earth. His advisers came back and said, "We don't have the technology, the know-how, or the money." Kennedy responded, "Make it happen." He voiced the possible, and it happened.

Similarly, Nelson Mandela was able to manifest a collective dream of the possible, bringing about extraordinary change against all odds. He transformed the division and hostility of apartheid into positive change and peaceful transition, with equality for all. Together, he and the people of South Africa achieved the most unlikely of destinies. If a few great men and women can change the fate of nations, imagine how much easier it is to change our individual fates.

The Momentum Tunnel

The momentum tunnel is the main channel of our time line, charting the events of our past, present, and future; in fact, 99 percent of our future possibilities can be extrapolated from the direction of its flow. These are the strands that lie inside the borders described by the solid cord of light extending from our past and into our future. And this is where 99 percent of the outcomes of our lives will fall.

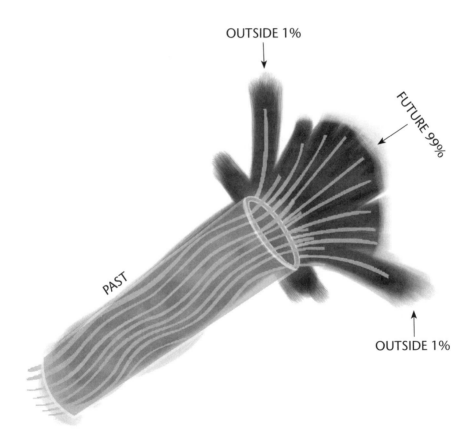

OUTSIDE 1%

FUTURE 99%

PAST

OUTSIDE 1%

Only one percent of our possibilities lies outside the momentum tunnel—these are the most difficult to achieve, but they're often the most promising. Certainly violence and dissent were more likely outcomes in South Africa than Mandela's peace; nonetheless, peace prevailed. Whites and blacks both had to make huge sacrifices and live with tough economic and social choices—in other words, they had to step outside the momentum tunnel. Once the difficult choices were made, the momentum tunnel lined up behind the country and supported it on its route to prosperity.

Our momentum tunnel is what keeps us going with the flow, executing the soul contracts we entered into when we were six, the genetic predispositions we inherited, and the choices we made before we were born. If we've already made the difficult choices that lead to wellness, longevity, and inner peace, then our momentum tunnel may already be supporting our journey. (This is what happens when we change the toxic relationship, leave the nightmare job, eat well and exercise, and have harmony in our life.) But for many of us who are in a more difficult place and wish to alter the course of our lives, the one percent that lies outside the momentum tunnel is where we can go to find our destiny. It's where we can look when our life isn't working and we need to explore other possibilities.

For example, when someone is diagnosed with a form of cancer that's fatal for the majority of people, 99 percent of their destiny lines may lead to a lengthy, crippling illness, or to death. Only one percent of the lines will lead to health, yet accessing this one percent requires them to change 99 percent of their life. Their genetics, lifestyle choices, and emotional environment all line up in the momentum tunnel leading toward disease, so they can go about changing their lives one aspect at a time (dieting, quitting a high-stress job, and so on); or, more powerfully, they can change the whole trajectory of their momentum tunnel energetically by journeying along their time line to select a more desirable destiny. This destiny is installed on their time line by the mere act of finding it and seeing it. The course of the momentum tunnel is then altered.

Once the course of the momentum tunnel lines up with your destiny, you can transform your entire life. You won't need to micromanage every choice you make, you'll merely need to be a good steward of the circumstances of your life, with the full knowledge and trust that the best destiny has already been selected. When destiny has been installed in your future, the universe conspires on your behalf to make it come true. Your inner-guidance systems direct you toward this destiny, and the hand of Spirit holds you.

Changing the Course of the Momentum Tunnel

Although changing the course of our momentum tunnel can be extremely desirable, it's often not an easy task. Imagine for a moment the difference between flying a Boeing 747 and a helicopter. A 747 is built so that your drink won't shake too much on the tray table in front of you—it's so smooth that you can take a nap, and the pilot can put the plane on autopilot, wander around the cabin, and chat with the passengers. But this stability comes at a price: To turn a 747, you have to make a wide sweeping motion that takes time, particularly if you want to do it so that none of the passengers find their drinks in their laps. This is how most of us design our lives—so that we can walk around on autopilot with a drink poised on a little table. But we pay a price. And, just like with the 747, it takes time to change course. We can't just wake up one morning and say, "I don't want to pay the mortgage anymore" or "I don't want to go to work anymore." Our lives aren't designed that way.

A helicopter is a totally different machine that's designed to turn on a dime and dart in and out of places quickly. It's great because you can touch down on tropical beaches and take off from the roof of a skyscraper, but you also have to be prepared to operate four controls at once, using both hands and feet. Forget about getting up and going for a stroll around the aircraft—all your attention needs to be focused on flying. You'll also have to jettison any excess baggage because a helicopter has to travel light. This means that the drinks, the meals, and the flight attendants will all have to go.

Here's a more mundane example. Let's say that you're driving 100 miles per hour in a pickup truck with a washer and dryer in the back, and suddenly you want to make a left turn. Even if you manage to make the turn at 100 mph, the washer and dryer will keep going forward, and you'll probably roll the truck over and go off the road. In order to make the turn safely, you need to slow way down. The problem is that most of us don't know how to slow down the truck—that is, how to cut back on our work hours or change our relationship with our children—because we've lost control of the momentum that propels us forward. If we don't jettison our baggage, then the washer and dryer, the job, the spouse, and even our health will be stripped from us.

Steve's New Destiny

Steve was a high-ranking scientist on a fast career track, working with the Stanford University Linear Accelerator. His team was investigating what happened in the third nanosecond after the big bang. They wanted to determine if there was enough matter in the universe for it to continue expanding for eternity, or if it was going to begin contracting into a reverse big bang. This was Steve's dream job.

When I met him, I asked, "What's the verdict for the universe: Are we expanding? What's the prognosis?"

He replied, "It looks good for the universe, but it doesn't look so good for me. I've just been diagnosed with a very aggressive kind of cancer, and I've done the research—98 percent of the people who get this disease die within four months."

Steve's former spouse had passed away sometime ago, and he had two young daughters whom he was raising by himself. He'd met the love of his life a few months earlier, but now he'd been handed a death sentence. Given the medical prognosis, 98 percent of the destiny lines in Steve's momentum tunnel led to death, death, and more death—only 2 percent lay outside of that tunnel, and half of *those* lines showed a possibility of serious illness. Only a minute percentage of Steve's destiny lines pointed to a healthy outcome. But Steve had a lot of reasons to live, so we had to track through that 2 percent window to find a future healed state that could begin to inform him.

Steve and I journeyed along his time line and discovered his healed self. Once we did, his future self guided him to health . . . but it required that he change his entire life. He had to give up his successful career, because the stress from his job was literally killing him. He had to let go of the "washer and dryer"—that is, the job at Stanford, the cutting edge of physics, accelerating nuclear particles, the publish-or-perish race, and the glory of his scientific accomplishments. He had to take up a life that supported his new, healed destiny.

Steve embraced this new destiny line outside his momentum tunnel, and jettisoned 98 percent of his former life in order to keep the essential 2 percent, which was life and love (not a bad trade-off!). He became a wood-carver and moved with his family to Alaska. Six months later, I performed his wedding ceremony.

Exercise: Mapping Your Time Line

In the following exercise, you'll learn the landscape of your own momentum tunnel. It's important to approach this exercise with an open mind. Destiny isn't always what we feel we want to change—certainly Steve wasn't interested in giving up his career as a physicist. But sometimes we truly need to change our lives, no matter how accomplished or successful, in order to have a healed and meaningful existence.

To begin, take a sheet of paper and draw four parallel lines going from left to right on the page. These are lifelines, along which you'll chart your personal and family history. On the first line, you'll plot those you've loved and when you loved them; these are your mad crushes, your sexual partners, your spouses, flirtations, and strong platonic friendships. Chart the names and the dates along this line.

On the second line, chart your emotional challenges. These can be bouts of uncertainty or depression, times of great happiness, or even stretches of time when you can't recall your mental state.

On the third line, chart the jobs you've had and the careers you've explored. On the fourth line, chart your personal and family health history; these are illnesses you've had, or those from which your parents, grandparents, and aunts and uncles suffered.

Take a look at these lines, and compare them. Look for patterns: Do you end relationships just as they're about to become truly intimate? Do you sabotage yourself just as you're about to succeed at something? What was happening with your relationships, career, and emotions when you developed health problems? What are the positive and negative trends you see?

These strands—love, power, money, and health—are the four key time lines in your life. Woven into a rope at the core of your momentum tunnel, they're the solid cordon of light on which the principal events of your past have been recorded. This is the fate that has been spun for you by your soul contracts.

In the next chapter, you'll learn to identify the limiting beliefs that keep you bound to these lines of fate. Then, in the chapter after that, you'll actually find your destiny lines—the lines of possible, not probable, futures—and track them to the greatest rewards and opportunities.

CHAPTER TEN

Sacrificing Sacred Cows

Three days upstream from the nearest jungle port, if you could even call it that. . . .

I swore I would never go to the jungle again, but that will teach me to never say never. Part of me remained behind in the mist and tangle of the Amazon when I experienced my own death, but I held on, cringed, and did not let go. That was three years ago. Now I know that I must return to go through that portal that most of us only get to go through at the end of our lives.

I've already seen what lies on the other side. I know that I must die to everything I believe in so that I can truly live.
— from Alberto's journal

Throughout time, human beings have looked upward for answers. This is why so many of our mythologies bring us to high places: The Shinto priests of Japan scale Mount Fuji; Turkey's Mount Ararat is revered by the Kurds; in India, Mount Arunachala is considered the embodiment of the Hindu god Shiva; the American Hopi kachinas revere Mount Blanca in Colorado; and, of course, the Greek gods lived and reigned on Mount Olympus.

With so many of our most sacred places being the highest points on Earth, it's no surprise that legends from around the world are filled with stories of the arduous journeys required to gain access to them—perhaps the best known being the biblical tale of Moses climbing Mount Sinai to receive the Ten Commandments. Sometimes our highest peaks even bear the marks of the immortals themselves. For example, on Adam's Peak in Sri Lanka, a gigantic fossilized footprint is thought to have been created by Adam after he was exiled from the Garden of Eden.

Now, while we mortals live in the Middle World of *Homo sapiens,* the Upper World is the domain of the *Homo luminous*—the realm of Spirit. This is the celestial terrain of angels and archangels, and of enlightened ones who are free from time and death. The Upper World is where you attain your divine nature, yet it's also where you discover the beautiful agreements that you made with Spirit before you were even born. Here, you'll learn about the true plot of your life—why you've come here to live, whom you are to love, and what you are to learn—you'll recall the agreements your soul made before you reentered the stream of time with your birth. These are the sacred agreements that you want to remember and start to live by.

Legends tell us that journeying to the Upper World is the hero's journey. So, if you want to reach the highest peaks, you must climb them as if you were a hero yourself. Being the flip side of the victim, the hero is able to respond to her calling in the face of insurmountable odds, while the victim is at the mercy of fate. Just as Psyche had to make it through arduous trials before ascending to Mount Olympus, you can only attain your destiny after going through a cleansing, purging, and purification process of your own. The myths teach us that you can only reach the peaks of the Upper World in a healed state, free of the demands of the ego and filled with grace and integrity.

Mayan prophets foretold of a new humanity being born from the ranks of the Upper World in the year 2012. This evolution of human beings will involve you, as you'll be a part of a quantum leap into becoming a new human species that will grow new bodies that will age, heal, and die differently. In your journey, you're going to learn that you will, in fact, experience this leap.

Sacred Cows

You can prepare yourself for your journey to the Upper World by ridding yourself of limiting beliefs about love, power, money, and health, such as: "I'm not good enough," "I don't deserve it," "Soul retrieval won't work for me," or "I'm too burdened by responsibility to change." Other versions are: "When the kids grow up, I'll change," "I'll practice yoga when I have more time," or "When I have enough money, I won't work so hard—and I'll eat better, too."

We hold on to these limiting beliefs, or "sacred cows," because we think that they'll provide us with security, but in reality they prevent us from achieving the one thing that will allow us to experience the magic of the world. We convince ourselves that if we get rid of the sacred cow, then we'll have nothing left. In other words, we think it's better to hang on to what little we've got than to have nothing at all: Better a bad relationship than no relationship; better a bad job than no job.

For example, one of my sacred cows used to be my fear of not being able to support my children. I kept telling myself, "When my children are grown, *then* I'll dedicate myself more fully to my calling as a writer and a healer, but for now, I have to do the responsible thing and work at the university." One day when my children were still little, I left the university and headed into the Amazon. It was on this trip that my mentor asked, "Alberto, do you want to live like an eagle or like a chicken?"

Of course I didn't want to live like a chicken! But there's a lot to be said for having the security of regular feedings in a chicken coop, as well as for the barbed wire that keeps out the fox. It's the barnyard equivalent of the corporate job with a retirement plan, or in my case, a university teaching position with a regular salary. But I also knew that many of us leave the chicken coop only to remain stuck on the ground of the barnyard—that is, we look longingly back at the coop, lacking the courage to take off and fly.

I had to face the fact that if I wanted to soar with the eagles, then I had to make some changes in my life. I had to give up the security of a teaching position to pursue my studies in the Amazon. At the time, I was one of the youngest members of the university's faculty, and I had a promising future in academia ahead of me. My decision meant sacrificing everyone's expectations of me, along with all the ones I had for myself.

However, after a few challenging years, my new career took off, and I was able to provide for my family with abundance. I no longer taught at the university, but I began lecturing around the world. My sacred cow had been hindering my ability to experience true success.

Letting Go of Limiting Beliefs

A sacred cow is the last thing that you want to lose or give up, and it might be something that you think absolutely must be maintained. For instance, I was once called in to consult with a company because its founder felt that the business was stagnating. He told me that he was willing to change any- and everything to improve the situation.

Well, after meeting with all his managers, I discovered that *he* was what had to be changed! The managers knew that the company was in trouble, but they were afraid to tell the boss about their difficulties with his management ideas. The company's founder was the sacred cow that had to be sacrificed in order to make any significant change.

I broke the news to the president: He had to fire himself. He ended up promoting himself to the board of directors and relinquishing day-to-day operations to a new generation. After that, the company began to flourish, and the employees were happier and thus more creative and productive. And the founder was able to return to the big-picture thinking and strategic planning that he'd always loved. He felt more fruitful and was rewarded with the joys of business partnership for the first time in his working life.

You see, a sacred cow is the limiting belief that we confuse with reality. It's always the one thing that we don't have the time, money, health, or courage to do, yet we must be willing to attempt in order to become whole. It's the thing that keeps us doing what we've always done for much longer than we should, even when we know it's wrong. As a client once told me, "My job is a nightmare, but I need the sleep." Even though he hated going to work, this man clung to his position, choosing to sleepwalk through life rather than risk exploring what it would be like to sacrifice this sacred cow and plunge into the unknown. Yet even though the risks are often enormous, the risks of sleepwalking through life are even greater.

When we cling to our limiting beliefs, illness or hardship may result. An acquaintance of mine who's a university professor kept telling me that when his retirement plan was fully funded, he'd finally do the things he wanted to do. Unfortunately, before that could happen, he died of a heart attack. The lesson here is that you can't always wait: You have to let go of your limiting beliefs so that you can journey to your destiny.

Of course this is easier to say than to actually do. I'm reminded of an old Indian story about a group of parrots who are in a cage at the palace of a sultan. An old bird tells the others (who were born in captivity) about the blue skies and how delicious the mangoes are when you eat them from the treetops, and how great it is to soar free beneath the clouds. One day, the bird-keeper accidentally leaves the cage open, and the storytelling bird says, "Go, my friends. Go and fly. Greet the treetops for me." One by one, all of the parrots fly out of the cage—except the one who talked them into it. This old bird just wasn't willing to sacrifice safety for freedom.

Limiting beliefs are always held as dogma. For example, the Italian astronomer Galileo was brought before the Inquisition in the 17th century as a heretic for supporting Copernicus's theory that the earth orbits around the sun, which was directly in conflict with the teachings of the time. This poor astronomer was criticized by a world that didn't know its proper place in the heavens, so he abandoned his investigations of the movement of celestial bodies for years after he was reprimanded by the Church. Nevertheless, he felt compelled to go back to his calling, defending it even before the Pope.

Galileo had to sacrifice the sacred cow that claimed our planet was the center of the universe, with the sun and stars spinning around it nightly. Even though he was kept under confinement for challenging this belief, by staying true to his destiny in the face of overwhelming danger he made discoveries that forever changed the course of science. Galileo's ideas were held to be false at the time—yet today they're universally accepted, and schoolchildren everywhere learn about him and his discoveries.

Just like Galileo, if you want to scale the highest heights, you must do so even in the face of rigid dogma and adversity. Your friends and family won't believe that you're leaving the job, career, or relationship they consider perfect for you—they'll think that you're following a fool's call. Yet answering your calling means that you only answer to one person's opinions: *yours*.

The Call of Destiny

It's possible that you may receive a calling to a destiny that even you'd rather ignore. It's tempting to say, "I'm not ready to do this yet—I'll do it at some other time. I'm comfortable now." But when you don't respond to a calling, you risk the wrath of heaven.

In the story of Jonah and the whale, for instance, God calls to the poor shopkeeper and says, "I want you to go to Nineveh." And Jonah responds, "No, I just want to have a simple life. I want to be a shopkeeper, and I want to be around my children and my grand-children." Jonah ignores his calling, gets on a ship, and sets off in the opposite direction from Nineveh. A huge storm rises, and the sailors know that someone has incurred the wrath of God. Crestfallen, Jonah admits to his fellow seafarers that he's the one who has done so. To save themselves, his shipmates throw Jonah overboard, and he's then swallowed by a whale that transports him in its belly to the shores of Nineveh anyway.

While in the belly of the whale, Jonah recognizes that his calling is to spread the word of God. When the humble shopkeeper is regurgi-tated by the whale in Nineveh, he then begins to teach—but he had to go through immense hardship before accepting this calling. Jonah's story teaches us that if we don't respond to our destiny of our own free will, we're going to be taken there anyway.

The call of destiny is an otherworldly one. It's not a menu choice between chicken and fish—it's a force entirely beyond our control. But we do still have the choice: Do we respond to the call of destiny on our own, or do we wait until an illness or personal crisis compels us to stop what we're doing and follow our destiny?

For many years I wanted to avoid my own calling. Every time I told myself, "I just want to have an ordinary job and a regular life," circumstances would conspire to bring me back to teaching and healing—I'd get sick, or the career I'd planned for myself wouldn't work out. I discovered the old adage that said, "If you want to see God laugh, make plans."

Accepting my own calling was always fraught with challenges—I had to face many fears and difficulties. For instance, after my first book, *The Realms of Healing,* was published, my co-author and I were chastised by the ethics committee of the American Psychological Association for promoting primitive "superstitions." Many of my colleagues believed that I was wasting my time studying "unconventional" healing, and even my own mother would ask me when I was planning to get a job. In the end, none of this mattered: I *had* to listen to my calling.

As you can tell, the call to your destiny doesn't always come in the way you expect it. For example, President Franklin Delano Roosevelt grew up in highly privileged circumstances and lived a life of success before being struck down with polio at the age of 39. But it was only after he was stricken with the disease that he embraced his destiny and achieved greatness on the world's stage. Aside from becoming one of our most effective and long-serving Presidents, Roosevelt also put in place a grassroots campaign that funded the discovery of a vaccine for polio, which stopped transmission of the disease that crippled him and was then terrorizing the country. Roosevelt didn't succumb to the belief that because he was disabled, he was powerless; to the contrary, he set in motion a healing that was far greater than his own personal illness. Roosevelt took a crippling condition and turned it into a healing crusade for others, transforming him from a man of privilege to a man of destiny.

There are many other such stories of people facing extraordinary obstacles and overcoming them, or of turning challenges into opportunities. Just think of Helen Keller, who was both deaf and blind, yet overcame her handicaps to learn how to read and communicate, and eventually became the first deaf and blind student to graduate from an American university. She went on to tour the country, inspiring thousands of deaf people to learn to communicate at a time when people with such disabilities were considered mentally ill.

Great individuals show us that we can sacrifice our limiting beliefs to change the nature of the quest from mere survival to destiny. So, what *is* your destiny? Is it getting accustomed to your limitations, or is it to change the world? The way of the healer has always been to discard limiting beliefs and turn them into sources of strength and inspiration. When you sacrifice your sacred cows, you no longer have any excuses that you can give to Spirit. There's no longer a disability to surmount before you can be of service to the world, or a child to rear before you can become a writer. There is only the resounding *yes* that you say to life.

Exercise: Identifying Your Sacred Cows

In this exercise, you'll identify and shed some of those limiting beliefs that keep you from living your destiny. You'll do this for each of the four strands that are woven into your momentum tunnel: your love relationships, power, money and career, and health. For each strand, fill in the blanks in the following sentence: When I _____ , then I will be able to _____. Be as specific as possible, and be honest.

Here are some examples of answers you might come up with:

- *Love relationships*
  When I find the right relationship, then I will be able to:
    — be happy
    — be fulfilled
    — stop feeling lonely
    — feel lovable

- *Power (psychological and emotional strength)*
  When I get over my anger at my mother, then I will be able to:
    — accept my daughter as she is
    — be more in touch with my femininity
    — have confidence
    — be open to meeting a man

- *Money and career*
  When I find the right job, then I will be able to:
    — learn to meditate and practice it daily
    — be more peaceful and contented
    — travel
    — become an accomplished chef

- *Health*
  When I'm not suffering from chronic fatigue, then I will be able to:
    — exercise regularly
    — learn to cook healthy meals
    — deal with my unhappiness
    — become active and fit

Look back at your answers. The first blank in the sentence is the sacred cow, the limiting belief that keeps you from advancing in life, while the second blank is the journey that you must be willing to embark on, whether or not the first blank occurs.

Despite the simplicity of the exercise, this tool is very revealing of your limiting beliefs. Since you have a whole herd of sacred cows, this exercise should be repeated often, delving deeper each time to reveal your most deep-seated beliefs. Used rigorously, this exercise will provide a doorway to your destiny.

Now that you've identified your sacred cows—and are willing to sacrifice them—you're ready to map the Upper World and meet your celestial parents.

CHAPTER ELEVEN

Journeying to Retrieve Your Destiny

There are two kinds of travelers: those who carry maps, and those who do not. When I was young, I was one of the latter kind. One day, I strayed off the trail deep in the rain forest (I knew I was only an hour away from camp)—two days later and no trail in sight, I kept repeating to myself, "You are not lost; lost is a state of mind. You simply do not know where you are."

On the third day, I finally admitted I was lost. Then I found a small stream. Nothing more than a trickle of water, really. But I knew it would lead to a tributary and then to the Amazon. I walked along the sandy bottom for two days until I reached the great river. Then I got a lift to port from two Indians in a motor-ized canoe who asked if I was lost.

"No," I said, "I'm simply finding myself." They smiled and didn't say another word.

There are those who follow maps, and those who make them.

— from Alberto's journal

Jonah's destiny took him to the shores of Nineveh even when he tried to run away. Just like him, you have a choice: You can wait until you're swallowed by a whale (or startled by the turn your life has taken), or you can take a more conscious path. Jonah was no dif-ferent from people who keep multitasking in their car—they speed to get to work on time as they chat away on their cell phone, while at the same time they drink coffee to stay awake because they never get enough sleep—until they're in a horrible, near-fatal accident. Life stops them cold and delivers them to another place, spitting them out on a "distant shore." After the accident, they're irrevocably changed, and questions of meaning and purpose dominate their existence.

The literature concerning near-death experiences is filled with such stories; that is, of people who were incredibly transformed after such an extraordinary incident. They tell of traveling through a dark tunnel before coming into the light. Here they encounter angelic beings, their celestial parents, who guide them in reviewing the events of their life, leading them to an understanding of its meaning and purpose.

In fact, the transformative power of a brush with death is one of the most popular themes in books and movies. For example, Charles Dickens wrote of Ebenezer Scrooge, who found a road of benevolence after a glimpse of his own mortality; and in the classic movie *It's a Wonderful Life,* the suicidal George Bailey is guided back to the meaning of his life by an angel-in-training, who shows him what the world would be like if George had never lived.

But why wait for an accident, an act of desperation, or the final moments of your life to learn the meaning of your existence? Why not experience that knowledge while you can still live with greater purpose? As the saying goes, nobody ever lies on their deathbed wishing that they'd spent a few more hours at the office. What we end up regretting is lost love, a lack of time with our children, or the absence of any meaningfulness in our lives. We regret not doing what would have given us a sense of emotional or creative fulfillment, a sense of having followed our calling.

Let's have this experience now—of going through the dark tunnel and coming out into the light, where we're guided by heavenly beings to the plot of our lives—without the traumatic event that *forces* us into consciousness. Let's journey to the Upper World, which is inhabited by our celestial parents, and experience the light today.

Navigating the Upper World

The Upper World is what psychiatry refers to as the *superconscious,* a realm that's greater than the limited ego sense we have in our everyday existence. When we journey to the Upper World, we enter this collective superconscious with access to our personal destiny, along with the destiny of our family or village or the piece of the earth over which we have stewardship—whether that be a garden, a farm, or a neighborhood in New York City.

All traditional societies refer to the Upper World (as do many religions), and each has its own map to describe the terrain. There are the Christian depictions of purgatory and paradise, which delineate the levels of purification humans must undergo before entering into paradise. There are the ancient maps of Tibet that illustrate the *bardo* planes, where a person's soul atones for his mistakes and then returns to the light after much hardship and suffering. And the Laika tell of a multitiered landscape (not unlike what the Tibetans believe), which is inhabited by the collective souls of minerals, plants, and animals, as well as the souls of our ancestors; and each of the five planes of this world exists in a different relationship to time. This is the map that we'll be following closely in this chapter.

The Laika, like many other religions, believe that after your death, you naturally gravitate toward one of these levels of the Upper World based upon how you've lived your life. If you arrive in an unhealed state, for instance, you're consigned to the lower tiers, where you undergo a period of cleansing and purging. Yet if you live consciously, you can arrive at one of the higher tiers of the Upper World, where there's no time or suffering . . . only joy.

The beings you're going to meet in the Upper World will welcome you and guide you to find the sacred contracts that you agreed to before you were born. These are beautiful agreements that you've ignored or didn't know how to recognize in your lifetime because you were blown off your course by trauma, ambition, or your expectation of how you should lead your life. In the Upper World, you're given the opportunity to ask your celestial parents how you can begin to live these sacred contracts right away, and how they can guide you toward your greatest fulfillment.

All of the steps you've gone through in the course of this book have been a preparation for this journey: You've used the soul-retrieval process to heal your past and recover your grace; you've explored your time lines to discover the toxic patterns that have kept you within your momentum tunnel of love relationships, power, health, and career; and you've sacrificed your sacred cows to release yourself from your limiting beliefs. These healing techniques have prepared you for the journey to the Upper World and will allow you to arrive there in a healed state, free to explore the possibility of destiny lines that lie outside your momentum tunnel.

The Five Planes of the Upper World

Before we begin, I'd like you to keep in mind that this is a sacred journey requiring proper precautions. Just as you did in the journey to the Lower World, you must open sacred space and pay your respects to the gatekeeper who guards the entrance to the Upper World. (In Christianity, the gatekeeper is the Holy Spirit, represented by a dove of fire; while in Judaism, it is the messiah.)

Now let's explore each level in depth.

The First Plane: The Level of the Stone People

Once you pass the gatekeeper, you'll enter into the lowest tiers of the Upper World. In the first level, time passes in a fashion similar to how you experience it in your world. It marches forward, taking the occasional detour to reverse itself, as it does in dreams, but it is basically linear.

This level is an earthbound world of darkness and suffering, where you purify yourself before moving on to higher levels that are filled with joy and peace. For indigenous cultures, the first level of the Upper World is known as the domain of the Stone People. This is where the essence and spirit of stones reside and energy vibrates at a very low frequency. In other words, it's a perfectly nice place if you happen to be a stone, but it's not all that great if you're a human. There's no light, there are no senses—you have a vague awareness of the presence of others, but you can't relate to them or communicate with them. Here, there is only suffering.

When we speak about an earthbound spirit that's purging and cleansing and is still attached to a place where it might have lived or was killed, we're referring to a spirit that's stuck in the realm of the Stone People. These are spirits that cling to the location of an automobile accident, a rape, or a murder—in other words, a place where soul loss and life loss happened at the same time. A soul may also become bound to a person whom she loved or hated, lingering and clinging to him until this other person joins her in the first tier, and they're able to resolve their souls' business together.

According to legend, you can't leave the first tier until you learn the ways of stewardship of the earth, represented by the Stone People. If you die with a lot of unresolved conflicts and relationships, for instance, you can get caught in this first level until you've said "I love you" and "I forgive you" to those you didn't share these statements with while alive. Such unfinished business can include wounds that haven't healed or transgressions that you've committed against another person or against nature. This is akin to the Christian concept of purgatory, where penance is made for a period of time before passing on to heaven, or to the Buddhist first world of the bardo, where you "do time," suffering and purging before you're able to pass into the timeless realms.[1]

The Second Plane: The Level of the Plant People

As a soul purges and heals, it becomes increasingly awake; consequently, it may pass into the second tier of the Upper World. This level is much more pleasant for humans than the first. You can see, and all of your senses are available to you, but there continues to be suffering as you purge from your last lifetime. In this plane, the tide of time still exerts a pull, and cause and effect still predominate.

Here, the many streams of your previous lifetimes run into the currents of your most recent existence. You not only recapitulate and experience the events of your recent past, but those of many other incarnations as well. You meet beings you recognize and who recognize you. As in a dream, people from the distant past and from your recent lifetimes appear and seek forgiveness or vengeance. You can interact with them, but as in dreams, scenes change rapidly and it takes a long time to find resolution.

According to legend, you can't leave the second tier until you accept responsibility for the stewardship of all green life, of the flowers, and of the forests. This is the domain of the Plant People, and although it's still a level of cleansing, it's also one of growth, life, and sunlight—it's a green world where the spirits of the plants reside. In Hopi mythology, this is the place where, after the coming of the light, plant life appears on the earth.

The Laika journey to this place to receive guidance as to which herbs and plants they should use for a person in need. It's from communing with this world that pharmacology first emerged among traditional peoples—it wasn't through trial and error, as we Westerners often believe. The healers didn't test a hundred remedies to see which one worked on a stomachache or a wound from an arrow. Today, when an ethnobotanist asks people in the rain forest how they know which plants to use in which combinations for any particular purpose, the answer from the shaman is simple: "The spirit of the plants tells us."

The Third Plane: The Level of the Animal Spirits

The third tier of the Upper World is the animal-spirit world, where the spirits of ancient creatures still roam. This domain is populated by the spirits of the elk, the eagle, the raven, the salmon, and the jaguar; but it's also where you'll find the spirits of all extinct species, such as the saber-toothed tiger, the mastodon, and the prehistoric whale. Just as you can journey to the second tier to receive the gifts of the spirits of the plants, you can do the same here in the animal-spirit world.

Even though it's a more elevated level, this plane is still not "home" for human beings. Individuals aren't differentiated from each other, and there's nothing but a complete absorption with nature, because animals have collective souls, unlike humans who have individual souls. There's no consciousness, no separation from anything that occurs around you—instead, you're absorbed and possessed by the collective, with no sense of "I," or self. Time is completely fluid in this world, although there's still a past and present.

The human souls that inhabit this world are in their final stages of purging. All that's required now is that they awaken and realize that they're dreaming. According to legend, you may not leave this tier until you can participate consciously in the evolution of *all* life.

Note that as you pass through the three natural domains of the Upper World, you may find the spirits of your ancestors, but you cannot contact them. You might meet your grandfather or an old friend in one of these domains, but they won't respond. This isn't where you commune with your departed loved ones, because they're occupied with purging and are inaccessible to the living. They can't hear you, and you can't offer them assistance. They might feel your love and your compassion, but they won't be able to perceive you. Now, although there are healers who specialize in assisting these beings, these souls have to go through their own process of forgiveness and atonement before they can find grace and be accessible to other humans in the fourth tier of the Upper World.

The Fourth Plane: The Level of Ancestors

The souls of your ancestors reside in the fourth tier, and you can engage them in dialogue because they've finished their own atonement process. This domain is filled with people, places, and things that mirror and parallel those from your world. Here you can meet your loved ones who have completed the journey back "home." (This is not unlike the passage in *The Divine Comedy* in which Dante is led through paradise by Beatrice, the attractive girl who lived near him in Florence, and who serves as the poet's ladder to godliness.)

Everything you've done thus far has been to heal your past now, while you still have a physical body, which will help you avoid the long and arduous journey through the lower planes of the afterlife. It's all been preparation for meeting your celestial parents, who will help you choose the next family you'll be born into, the circumstances and place of your next birth, and what kind of life experiences you'll have in your next incarnation. You see, your soul exerts a tremendous gravitational force on the family it wishes to be born into, even bringing lovers together for a single night of romance in order to be born to those parents.

Your celestial parents will remind you of the reason that you were given life, and they'll restore to you the terms of the original sacred contract with Spirit that you entered into. Although these great beings are referred to as "parents," they're not your biological ancestors—instead, they're benevolent archetypes who are free of the psychological and genetic baggage that your human parents handed over to you. They're your *spiritual,* not *physical,* lineage, and they guide you without judgment or expectation, welcoming your soul home, and helping you reestablish your original destiny. As Raymond Moody, one of the foremost investigators of near-death experiences, once wrote, the feelings of being judged "came not from the being of light, who seemed to love and accept these people anyway, but rather from within the individual being judged."[2]

The life-review process occurs in the presence of your celestial parents, and this is where you're the accused, the defendant, the judge, and the jury all at once. This is where you render your accounts as to how you've been true to your original soul contract: How faithful have you been to what you came to learn? How did you come to experience love and to serve? In the same way that your biological parents deliver you into this world, your celestial parents deliver you into the next, welcoming you home after your death.

The fourth tier is a realm of peace and rest for humans, where souls gather between incarnations. Even though you've purged and atoned, your soul's history will determine your next incarnation. Time stands nearly still, but cause and effect and the law of karma still predominate. A minute in this realm can be a century of Earth time. And according to legend, you don't evolve beyond this domain until you accept responsibility for dreaming the entire universe into being. (I'll detail this concept in the next chapter.)

The Fifth Plane: The Level of the Highest

From the fourth tier, you can climb a ladder into the fifth and highest level of the Upper World. This is the realm of the angels and archangels, where the great medicine healers reside. This is where all the souls dedicated to assisting humankind dwell, including the bodhisattvas of Buddhism and the saints of Christianity. This is where you meet your self that never entered the stream of time, the one containing all the knowledge of the person you're evolving into.

Although this notion of "climbing a cosmic ladder" might seem strange, representations of this ladder can be seen sticking out of underground kivas and pointing toward the sky all over the American Southwest. In the Inka tradition, this ladder leads to Sirius, the Dog Star, and then into the Upper World. Another metaphor for climbing this ladder is arriving at the pinnacle of a mountain where you can easily see the valley and the fields of your life below you with great clarity. (You'll learn more about this fifth tier in the next chapter.)

Visiting the Upper World Now

Although all five domains are available to you after your death, they can also be visited while you're living—through journeying.

If you journey to the Upper World now, you can ask your celestial parents to remind you of how you can live according to your original sacred contract in this lifetime. You can reinstate its original terms and explore the ways in which you may want to revise it. You can ask them to guide you through a process of reflection on how true you've been to your sacred contract and how you've served it (or neglected to). When you forget these sacred contracts, you begin to believe that life is about spending 60 hours a week at the office, then arguing with your mechanic over a rough idle in your car . . . all the while suspecting that these issues have nothing to do with why you were put on this planet.

This will be your life-review process, and your celestial parents will help you find resolution and atonement for all the ways in which you've deviated from your original sacred contracts. In the process, they'll set you on a journey of meaning and purpose for the rest of your life.

Let me give you an example from my own life that illustrates how valuable this journey can be, as well as how much our celestial parents can facilitate our understanding. On one journey, my celestial parents led me to meet my biological father, who had passed away several years earlier. I was delighted to see that he wasn't suffering and that he was joyous and filled with light. He hugged me, looked into my eyes, and said, "Until you realize why you were born my son, you will continue to live my life."

My father was a kind and loving man, but he was also a workaholic who missed out on much of the fun of life, so this encounter launched me on a three-year-long exploration of my family psychology and genetic predispositions to health and disease. One day I mentioned the details of this journey to one of my mentors, who pointed out that I'd made an error in punctuation when I transcribed my father's words—I was missing a comma. What my father had admonished me to understand was really this: "Until you realize *why you were born,* my son, you will continue to live my life." This launched me on a quest for my original contract, and for the meaning and purpose I'd chosen for this life.

In the Upper World, you'll have an opportunity to respond for the second time to your original calling. Like Parsifal when he meets the old hermit in the forest, removes his armor, and finds the Grail Castle for the second time, you'll also remember why you were born and what you came here to do in this lifetime. This may be a spiritual calling, a creative calling, or a calling to be of service. You may find that you're to be a poet, a sculptor, a healer, someone who can save a river or an endangered species, or simply a voice of compassion and understanding to those in need.

When you embrace your sacred contract, you'll be shown the possibilities of your destiny—its challenges, its wonders, its mysteries, and its inner power. If you fulfill this destiny, as challenging as it can be, after your death you'll arrive in the Upper World in a healed state, and you'll avoid the suffering of the lower domains, where the greatest sin is having been false to your original soul contract.

Remember: You journey to discover what's possible for your soul in this life and in the next. You journey to make sweeping changes, which can't be made in the small increments of daily life. You can't make these choices by reacting to where the stock market is today, or where you hope it will be tomorrow. You can't make them by gauging how your spouse is feeling today or how she might react if you make a change, or by obsessing on the opportunities you had last week but failed to take advantage of. The soul's choices are the great decisions that can only be made from the fifth plane, as you navigate through your destiny and express it in the now. In the Upper World, you'll be selecting your future—and all future incarnations to come.

The Cost of Transformation

Now, keep in mind that there's a cost for everything, and the "sticker price" for this transformation is that you have to realign your priorities and make fundamental changes. For example, if you choose material success over emotional and spiritual communion with others, you'll pay the price of suffering; yet if you alter your life to be more spiritual and emotionally invested, you're going to have to clean up your act. Nevertheless, *you always have a choice,* even in the living of your destiny.

You can go with the big house, the flashy car, and the multinational conglomerate, but you have to be willing to pay the price. Or you can choose a life of love and service, but you may not live in the lap of luxury . . . then again, you may not even notice, because when you live in the comfort of the soul, *all* comforts follow. The Laika call this *munay,* or "action from the heart," because the things you do from the heart have the least karma attached to them, and you don't have to mortgage your soul to obtain them.

This doesn't mean that you can't be materially successful—it simply means that worldly achievements aren't the sole measure of your success, just as shunning material wealth isn't the only measure of your spiritual growth. The following teaching story will illustrate this clearly.

Once there was a monk who lived by a river. Every day he would fish and give away his catch to the hungry—all he would keep for himself was a single fish head to make soup with in the evening. One day one of his students told the monk that he was traveling to the holy mountain. The teacher was overjoyed and asked the student to visit his old master to ask him for assistance. "Ask him why I am stuck in my spiritual practice," he said.

The traveler embarked upon his journey. When he reached the foot of the holy mountain, he inquired of an innkeeper, "Where does the master live?" The innkeeper answered, "He lives at the top of the mountain. The orchards that you see are his orchards. The herds of cattle are his. Those are his fields planted with wheat and barley." The traveler was stunned that a spiritual master would have such great wealth. As he made his way up the mountain, he stopped and spoke to one of the gardeners, who confirmed that indeed these were the master's orchards.

When he reached the top of the mountain, he found a magnificent castle. He knocked on the door, and the master's wife welcomed him in. As she offered him a feast such as he had never before seen, she informed him that her husband would be arriving later.

At sunset, the master arrived in a chariot drawn by four horses and attended by footmen. He welcomed the traveler and inquired of his old student. The traveler said, "He has begged me to ask you for help. He wants to know why he is stuck in his spiritual growth."

The master closed his eyes for a moment, and when he opened them again, he said, "Aha! It is because he is too materialistic." The traveler was sure the old master must be mistaken. But the master said, "No. Tell him what I said." And he bid the traveler a good journey home.

On his return, the traveler approached the fisherman monk and said, "I have news from your master, but there must be a mistake. He says that the reason you are stuck is because you are too materialistic."

The monk knew instantly that this was true. "Yes!" he exclaimed. "Of course!"

The traveler was mystified. "How can this be so?" he asked. "After all, you give everything away."

"This is the point," said the monk. "In the evening when I am cooking my fish-head soup, all I can think about is the rest of the fish." The master, on the other hand, knew that he was not consumed by his possessions or defined by the wealth he had.

It's Never Too Late

Destiny can come to you in many different ways—and it can even come at the end of your life. For example, Anne was a designer and artist who had very advanced liver cancer. She was under hospice care and had been given only a few days to live when her mother contacted me.

When I met Anne, her skin was yellow with jaundice, since her liver had nearly ceased to function, and she was in terrible pain and fear. Together, we journeyed to the Upper World, where we found her deceased grandparents. They held Anne's hand and assured her that there was nothing to fear, and that they were there to assist her in crossing to the spirit world and returning back home. Then she met her celestial parents, two beings of light who held her and told her not to be afraid. Immediately, Anne recognized one of them as her spiritual mentor, Swami Muktananda (an Indian master and teacher who died in 1982), who explained to her that her work was not yet done. On her return from this journey, Anne had a smile on her face and explained to me that she was no longer afraid.

Through a curious set of coincidences, I'd ended up with Muktananda's walking stick. It was engraved with the eye of the peacock feather, the Hindu symbol of grace, which the swami had taken as his personal symbol. On my next visit to Anne, I brought her the stick and told her that it had helped a great man walk this world, and it would help her cross into the next one. From that day on, Anne held the walking stick by her side at all times.

Within the next few days, Anne's jaundice began to clear, and she was dismissed from the hospice. A week later, she explained to me that her pain had diminished and her energy was returning, but that she was exhausted from healing her family, who had come from all over the country to be with her. For the last few days, Anne's work had been to get relatives to forgive one another and make peace.

Two weeks later, her mother called to tell me that the monarch butterflies were in the bushes outside Anne's deck. "They've come for her," she said. And that evening, Anne passed away peacefully.

This wonderful lady taught me that while we live in a body, we're subject to the laws of biology—that is, we can only install in our destiny line what's permissible in our universe. (We couldn't find Anne a new liver, for instance.) But by living within the laws of this universe, we can change many things. Miracles can and do happen, but only when we go seeking the spiritual gifts of the Upper World.

Anne retrieved her original soul contract to heal those she loved, and she was able to journey to her teacher. As I mentioned before, when you find your original soul contract and organize your life around it, the universe conspires to support it, as it did for Anne. She had enough time to do what she needed to do in this world, before she passed on to the next.

Guidance for Your Journey

In the exercise that follows, you'll journey to the Upper World, where you'll meet your celestial parents and ask them to reveal your original soul agreement. For this first journey, ask them a simple question, such as "How can I be of service?" or something specific to a project or a relationship. Avoid broader questions such as, "What should I do with the rest of my life?" There will be time on later journeys for these larger questions when you become more familiar with the terrain of the Upper World.

Right now, your job is to be open to the possibilities of your destiny, whatever it might be, and remember that you can only attain what is permissible in our universe. This might surprise or even shock you, for

Journeying to Retrieve Your Destiny

reality is even stranger than fiction. Yet we all have possibilities and capabilities beyond our wildest imaginations.

Before you leave the Upper World, you'll call out for a power animal whose instinct and qualities will guide you to your destiny. Even though it will serve a similar function to the one you received in the Lower World, the spirit animal that you're gifted from the Upper World is almost always a winged creature, such as a hawk, dove, or eagle. It will teach you vision and the ability to put your life into perspective.

Exercise: Journey to the Upper World

Prepare for this journey by opening sacred space. Perform the little-death exercise, and then silently state your intention for this journey: that you would like to meet your celestial parents.

Imagine a great tree in front of you, whose roots go deep into the earth, whose trunk is wide and spacious, and whose branches extend into the heavens. Send your luminous body into the trunk of this tree. Experience yourself within it, being held in its embrace, the sap flowing through you as it rises from the roots and up into the branches. Allow that sap to carry you to the uppermost branches, and come to a place above the clouds.

Look around you. You are on a solid cloud, and you can stand and walk safely. Now call on the gatekeeper: "Keeper of the Time to Come, you who make the stars turn on their orbits, allow me to enter your domains." See the gatekeeper approaching and welcoming you. Look into his eyes and state your intent again.

Ask the gatekeeper to bring you to your celestial parents. Notice how two lights approach from a distance and draw close to you. Greet them—these are your luminous parents, archetypes that are free from time and form. Sense how they greet you, saying, "Welcome home, my little one, all is well."

163

Ask these beings, "Who are you? Are you my celestial parents?" and "How are you related to me?"

As you commune with these luminous beings, notice how your thoughts and theirs become one. There is no separation between you. Anything you think, they perceive instantly and totally. Anything they think, you perceive in its entirety.

Ask these beings to remind you of that original sacred contract you agreed to before you came into this lifetime. Ask why you chose the parents you picked, the place you were born, and the circumstances of your birth. Ask them to remind you of the agreement that you made with Spirit before you were born: What did you come here to experience, explore, learn, and serve? How true have you been to this agreement? How do you reinstate its original terms?

Remembering your sacred contract, follow these two beings of light to a great ladder that's resting on the clouds. See how the top of the ladder extends above the sky, and follow them up into the fifth world, to the place of your becoming. Look about you: This is a place of diamond cities, of crystal villages, of unspoiled earth and pristine rivers. Ask that you be shown the destiny line that will bring you the highest good, where you will be of greatest service to all life. You may perceive this as a feeling, sensation, or image, or as words. But the important thing is to perceive it with your heart and soul.

Once you've perceived this highest destiny, inquire what your new sacred contract can be. Does it include your deep longings and aspirations? Ask your celestial parents what you are committing to learn, love, and experience. Remember that you can *negotiate the terms of this new agreement.*

Now begin your journey down the ladder, and back into the fourth world. If you like, take a moment to visit in the village of your ancestors, and know that all is well with them. When you've finished, thank your celestial parents, who will be waiting for you when you return back home after your death. Thank them for helping you remember your sacred contracts. And thank them for allowing you to bring back in your heart the destiny that you've retrieved.

As you prepare to leave the Upper World, thank the gate-keeper and call on a winged spirit animal to accompany you. Sense how it drapes its wings around you, holding you sweetly. Know that it is here to guide and protect you.

With your spirit animal, go through the clouds and into the uppermost limbs of the great tree, descending down the branches as they grow thicker and thicker, allowing the sap to carry you back down through the massive trunk. Feel the spirit animal coming with you, flying around you as you descend. Step out of the tree and back into the room and into your body.

Sense the spirit animal hovering about you. Look deeply into its eyes: What color are they? Feel its talons. Extend your hands and take this winged animal energetically into your seventh chakra. Feel it extend its wings inside your heart.

Come back into our world, bringing forth that which you retrieved, remembering who you are, where you come from, and what you came here to experience. Carry this intent in your heart with purity and compassion. Take a deep breath, open your eyes, and close sacred space.

Exercise: A Journal Dialogue with Your Celestial Parents

After you've journeyed, use your journal to engage in dialogue with your celestial parents and to learn the gifts of your winged power animal. These journal exercises can be conducted in the same way as those you've done with your lost soul parts and your power animals from the Lower World. The purpose is to create an ongoing dialogue with these archetypal beings as they reveal their energies. Ask for their lessons and to hear their voice.

Start by creating sacred space, and draw a line down the center of a blank journal page. On one side, you'll be asking questions of either your celestial parents or your winged power animal; on the other side, they'll answer. Begin by asking simple questions, but allow enough time for a full dialogue to emerge before closing sacred space.

Repeat this exercise to learn as much as they'll teach you. It's preferable to dialogue with your celestial parents and your power animal in separate exercises so that the voices don't crowd each other out. You want to be able to receive their wisdom without feeling that there's more information than you can absorb. Begin by holding this dialogue with your celestial parents. Ask them questions such as: "What did I come into this world to explore and experience?" "What lessons have I had to learn through suffering that I might have learned through love?" "What lessons do I still have to learn?" and "What gifts have I come to express?"

When you're done, repeat this exercise with your spirit animal.

Remember in your dialogue with your celestial parents that just because you may have embraced a new destiny, this doesn't mean that you'll necessarily understand all of its implications. Understanding follows healing—the mind gets things long after your heart and your body comprehend them. But even if you don't grasp it just yet, your body will have a reference for it, and you'll be able to find this destiny in your heart, and this will guide you to its fulfillment.

There will be a knowingness that comes from this journey: You'll realize, consciously or not, that a high destiny has been installed in your future time line. All you have to do is walk toward it. You no longer have to go through all the mind-befuddling choices and alternatives and options, but you can be guided by a choice that you've retrieved in your soul. The most essential part of you will know and remember, and it will help you surrender to this new path.

Exercise: Altar Building

In traditional societies, after the first few journeys to meet the ancestors, it's common to create an altar in their honor. Although anthropologists often speak of "ancestor worship," this is something very different: Altar building is a way of honoring and remembering your ancestors, and a way of coming to peace with them.

You build an ancestor altar so that they have a place to be and you know where they are—after all, you don't want them running amok through your life! A client of mine once had a relative who died in an automobile accident "move into" her car. Everywhere she drove her car, she'd feel the presence of this relative in the backseat. After she built her ancestor altar, her deceased relative found a place of peace and rest.

To build an altar to honor and remember your ancestors, place photographs of relatives who have already returned to Spirit on a shelf, perhaps on a favorite cloth. Light a candle for them on the anniversary of their death, and remember that they continue living, even though they're not among us anymore. On other occasions, you can burn incense or say a prayer asking that they bring peace and protection to your home.

In the next chapter, you'll learn how to clear the momentum tunnel from your former lifetimes. You'll help your former lives, who still exist in the Timeless Now, to move up to consciousness and peace in the fifth tier, freeing yourself from their karma.

CHAPTER TWELVE

Growing New Bodies

*"How do you apply quantum mechanics to everyday life?"
my mentor challenged. "Does quantum theory teach you how
to walk on the earth? How to change the weather?"*

*The secret follows from the mastery of invisibility and of
time. It is not the secret that is important, it is your ability to
keep this secret; it is how you hold it. Knowing it is like knowing
the future, and who but those who understand that time turns
like a wheel can manage to know the future and not let it upset
their balance? If your faith in reality is based on a belief that
time moves in one direction only, then the foundation of your
faith will be shattered by an experience of the future. This does
not concern the shaman, because the shaman has no need for
faith—the shaman has experience. Nevertheless, it takes great
skill to know the future and not allow your knowledge to spoil
your actions or your intent.*

— from Alberto's journal[1]

Louis Pasteur, the 19th-century French scientist who developed germ theory, held that the reason we become ill is because microbes invade the body—once they penetrate the protective barrier of the skin (or mucous membrane) in the sinuses or lungs, they contaminate our system. Yet Antoine Beauchamp, a contemporary of Pasteur, did not agree with this theory.

Beauchamp hypothesized that germs were present everywhere, all the time, and that it's the internal environment of the body— something that would later be termed *the immune system*—that determined how vulnerable we might be to disease. He observed that flies are attracted to garbage because it offers them a place to feed, but they certainly didn't *cause* the garbage; in fact, without it, they'd buzz off until they found somewhere else to feast. The same is true, he reasoned, with the human body: There must be some inherent condition in it that allows microbes to feast on us and cause disease or illness. So, Beauchamp can rightfully be called "the father of modern naturopathic medicine," which seeks to build a strong immune system so that regardless of what's in the atmosphere, one won't be afflicted by disease.

Toward the end of his life, Pasteur rescinded his position and agreed that the key to disease is indeed the internal environment of the body. Yet, despite his change of heart, germ theory has predominated to this day. It gave rise to pasteurization, a way of using heat to kill bacteria in your food supply (you only drink pasteurized milk, for example), and the development of antibiotics to attack and kill invading bacteria in the body. But antibiotics have had the unintended consequence of developing resistant strains of bacteria that have adapted to evade destruction by all but the most powerful formulas. When antibiotics were first introduced in the 1940s, 100 percent of *staphylococcus* was responsive to antibiotic treatment; today, 26 percent of all staph infections are resistant to any form of antibiotics, and staph-related infections acquired in hospitals are one of the leading causes of death in America.

As we invent stronger and stronger medications, we create stronger and stronger bacteria. It's doubtful that we'll continue to find new and more powerful antibiotics that the body can tolerate, so for now, the scoreboard reads "Germs: 1; Humans: 0." We're actually exhausting our antibiotic arsenals—in effect, bringing us nearer to the end of antimicrobial medicine as we know it.

The Blueprint for Healing

In contrast with Western medicine and its emphasis on killing microbes and cancer cells, there's an ancient school of thought that says that your health is determined by your proper relationship with nature. For the Laika, there's no difference between being killed by a microbe and being felled by a jaguar. While we in the West believe that one is an illness while the other is an accident, the Laika see them as identical problems that have to do with being out of harmony with the natural world. In order to thrive, you have to be in proper relationship with *both* microbes and jaguars so that neither will view you as lunch.

Thus, you're neither under perpetual siege, as a follower of Pasteur might think, nor invincible as long as you cultivate a robust immune system, as prescribed by Beauchamp. Instead, you only subject yourself to attack by predators when you're out of balance with nature.

The Laika call this balance *ayni,* which means "proper relationship" (that is, when you're in ayni, you coexist with jaguars and microbes without becoming part of their food chain). The origin of ayni is in the mythology of the indigenous Americans, which says that the universe is benign and will order itself to conspire on our behalf when we're in proper relationship with it. In Western mythology, we learn that we live in a predatory universe where there's an independent evil principle against which we must guard ourselves with holy water, amulets, prayers, and vaccinations. For the Laika, evil exists, but only in the hearts of men and women. All of creation is benevolent, and it only becomes predatory when we're out of ayni.

When we become ill, the first step is to come back into ayni; otherwise, no herbs or other medication will work effectively. Yet being out of alignment with nature is essentially the condition of the modern human: We've poisoned the environment, cut down the forests, and polluted the rivers; waged wars on microbes and other humans; pushed species into extinction by our predatory nature; and altered natural habitats to put in shopping malls. In other words, we've been behaving like a parasite that has attacked its host.

Our behavior is a form of matricide, in which the child of nature— the human—is killing its own mother. To protect herself, nature is beginning to reject us: Water supplies are drying up, new plagues are infecting the planet, and the earth is beginning to respond to us as an undesirable life form. We're becoming a flea on the tail of a dog, a germ that will be annihilated by the immune system of the planet.

All this comes at a time when medicine feels newly empowered by our discoveries of the secret of life. When Watson and Crick discovered the DNA code, we suddenly converted to a new scientific faith, and antimicrobial medicine became supplemented by genetics. We now believe that risk factors inherited from our parents and ancestors through our genes predispose us to how long we're going to live (and how well), what illnesses we're going to get, how we're going to heal, and how we're going to age. We've devised tests to tell us from birth what genetic risks we've inherited, and we race to find cures from the same DNA strands that we use to predict our future. Genetic markers, nanotechnology, and other tools of the biotechnology industry promise us healthier and longer lives.

But this is just a new trick for an old dog, because biotechnology is still looking for ways to fix, correct, and kill at an even subtler molecular level. We've simply added more precision and skill to the attack, while what we should be doing is seeking harmony with nature, both inside and out.

I teach my students that evolution happens *within* generations, not *in between* them, as is taught by traditional biology. Genetics tells us that we're warm, fuzzy carriers for our genes until they leap into the next generation, and the best we can hope for is to learn to live with the deficiencies that we've inherited.[2]

However, for the Laika, the blueprint is not in our genes, it's in the *luminous energy field* that envelops and organizes our physical body, in the same way that a magnet will organize iron filings on a piece of paper. This energy field has existed since the beginning of time, and it will endure throughout infinity, crafting new physical bodies lifetime after lifetime. It molds and shapes our body, and it predisposes us to meet the people we'll work with and marry, along with the crises and opportunities we'll encounter in our lives—it's what we in the West call "the soul."

Indian and Tibetan mystics who documented the existence of the luminous energy field thousands of years ago described it as an "aura" or "halo" around the physical body. In the East, the Buddha is shown in paintings with blue and golden bands of fire enveloping him; while in the West, Christ and the apostles are shown with golden halos around their heads. Yet these luminous fields aren't just the quality of Buddha and Christ, nor are they only a metaphor for an "inner light" or "enlightenment"—they describe a radiance we all have. Unfortunately for most of us, this luminosity has been dulled by our suffering and past trauma, but when we heal our luminous energy field through soul retrieval, our light will be restored and again shine with a brilliance like that of Christ or Buddha.

To visualize your luminous energy field, imagine that you're surrounded by a translucent, multicolored orb, which encircles you to the width of your outstretched arms. Within this orb is a living energy, as indispensable to your health as the oxygen and nutrients carried by your bloodstream—and the most astonishing memory bank ever created by nature.

By journeying to discover who you're becoming, your luminous energy field can be informed by a blueprint from the future. You can transform the field that surrounds you, and it will uncoil the DNA code another strand, catalyzing genetic change within your own generation. You can then pass on these new traits to your children, evolving the species within your lifetime and growing a new body that ages and heals differently.

Conscious Evolution

Despite the wide acceptance of the theories of genetic inheritance and natural selection, evolutionary biologists have observed that evolution works by taking quantum jumps, rather than baby steps, forward. They ask, for example, how reptiles evolved into birds—after all, they certainly didn't grow one feather at a time. An enormous leap occurred in which serpents grew wings, in which dinosaurs became flying reptiles, and in which whales left the oceans for a brief period to live on land. (This is known as *punctuated equilibrium,* or long periods of relative stability interrupted—or punctuated—by brief periods of extreme change.)

Evolution, these scientists theorize, also works through a process known as *quantum speciation,* whereby a small group or island population will take a quantum leap into the future and develop new biological characteristics or technological capabilities. For example, the famous "missing link" in evolution has never been found. This is because we became *Homo sapiens* in a few very rapid series of evolutionary quantum jumps, in which a whole new brain (the neocortex), appeared over a small number of generations.

At the same time, the changes resulting from quantum speciation are so extreme that it can take thousands of years for those new traits to be employed by the species as a whole. For example, while the neocortex—the brain of science, music, and literature—appeared in human beings nearly 100,000 years ago, it didn't become an active bio-computer until very recently.

"Quantum speciation" is an excellent way to describe the technique the Laika use in retrieving destiny. They throw a grappling hook into the future to see what we're becoming as a species, and then they retrieve that knowledge to inform their own luminous-energy field and those of the members of their village.

Today, the task of consciously guiding our evolution takes on a special relevance, particularly in the light of medical practices that have severed our connection to nature. We've broken away from the guiding hand of natural selection and have begun to self-select as a species. Where nature and evolution have always eliminated the less fit members of the species (through natural selection), we've dramatically decreased infant mortality rates in America from more than 15 percent to less than one percent, saving children that nature may not have otherwise elected to survive. While this is a wonderful statistic for families and societies, sparing the lives of weak and infirm children means that we deplete the gene pool by saving individuals who will transmit their medical problems to their offspring.

Now, although this concept sounds very esoteric, you can think of conscious evolution in mundane terms. As we look into the mirror on a daily basis, for instance, many of us recognize the signs of age approaching. Our skin cells are making new copies of themselves on a weekly basis—every cell is a copy of the generation before, replicating all the genetic instructions from its parent. Biologists sometimes compare the aging process of cells to making a photocopy of a photocopy: By the 99th copy, the image begins to grow fuzzy. So sometime in your late 30s, your skin begins to lose its elasticity, the crow's-feet around your eyes become more pronounced, and deep wrinkles begin to appear . . . if only you could make an exact replica of the original image, instead of copies of copies!

We see the effects of our bodies living in time, and we wish that we could step outside of it, if only for reasons of vanity. But there are tremendous opportunities inherent in the aging process. For example, not a single molecule that's inside your body today will be there next year—every atom is exchanged every eight months. The food you eat ends up sending elements and minerals into your cells via your bloodstream, so who you are today was salmon, corn, earth, and river a few days ago. In effect, you grow an entirely new body every eight months, swapping your molecular structure with that of the world around you. In eight months, those molecules that are in your body today will be tree, tomato, and ocean. This is a constant process of cellular renewal.

If you can tap in to the blueprint of who you're becoming, you can allow that template to re-create your body with the building blocks of nature: earth, air, fire, water, and light. This is akin to downloading the newest version of the "software of life" that can upgrade itself on a daily basis. Thus, you don't have to rely exclusively on DNA, the hardware that executes the genetic instructions in the body. The new program can supply guidance and wisdom for the luminous energy field to organize the body, according to the template of who we're becoming as a species.

Your Original Self

In the West, we believe that all life is predetermined by genetic inheritance from past generations. For the Laika, evolution is journeying into the future to see who we're becoming so that we may bring that knowledge back to the present. The Laika have always believed that it's the memories stored in our luminous energy field (the karma from our former lives) that determines our fate. This can only be healed in its entirety from the fifth world, where we find our perfect original self.

The first four levels of the Upper World represent four stages of awareness of your own nature. In the first stage, you experience God as outside yourself, which is common to most religions. In the second, you discover that God is within you through a process of self-inquiry. The classic question here is "Who am I?" and, later, "Who is it that's asking this question?" In the third stage, you experience God as working *through* you; while in the fourth, you discover God working *as* you. God is no longer working through you, there's only God working, playing, and praying.[3]

By journeying into the fifth world, you can find your original self, as well as who you'll be after you die. This self can inform you beyond your parents and your genes, drawing wisdom from your timeless self, and allowing you to access your possible destinies. (We're the first species to be able to do this, because we have a brain that's complex enough to step outside of time.) It remembers who you've been in all of your former incarnations, and it knows the forms, shapes, and histories that you've lived. Your original self knows that while you've lived all those lives, you're not those people. You are much more—you're God masquerading as yourself.

This fifth tier is also where the Laika go to consult the lineage of medicine men and women who guide them to their destinies. Similarly, they'll guide *you* beyond your genetics, ancestral, and personal histories, as well as childhood traumas and the cultures and beliefs with which you were raised. They'll steer you beyond your experiences from previous lifetimes to embody whom you're becoming, both as an individual and as part of the species. In the Timeless Now, you already are who you're becoming, and these medicine men and women help you realize this. Unlike the lower domains of the Upper World that are still bound to time, the fifth world is *completely* outside of it. It's as if you're sitting on the banks of a river that flows in all directions, and you can observe all of the future swirling by you.

Clearing the Momentum Tunnel

In the upcoming exercise section, your original self will help you clear the momentum tunnel from three former lifetimes, releasing you from the suffering that continues to inform you today. These are aspects of yourself that were trapped energetically in the lower tiers of the Upper World. As you heal these former lifetimes, they'll cease to actively compel and propel you toward prescribed destinies. You'll clear your karmic lines of reincarnation and drain their momentum so that you can be free of the unhelpful and unhealthy scripts that they bring with them from your history.

To drain the energy from the momentum tunnel, you must free your past selves from their suffering. This will stop them from informing you who you are today and predisposing you to live, age, love, heal, ail, and die in the ways that you have in the past. In this way, you'll discover that it isn't your genes or the germs that surround you that incline you to health, longevity, ailments, suffering, joy, and love. It is your soul's history . . . and its journey.

The work in this chapter requires a degree of emotional and spiritual sophistication. During soul retrieval, you learned to heal your past and understand the stories that live within you—but now you're going to come to the understanding that you're not your stories, just as the carpenter isn't the chair he builds. But you can only come to this realization after engaging in your own healing journey.

You'll ask to see the lifetime in which you suffered the most, the one in which you had the greatest knowledge and power but used your gifts poorly, and the one in which you had great wisdom and used your gifts well. And as you look at these lifetimes, you're going to drain the energy from each of these former lives. You'll even do this for the lifetime in which you used your gifts well, because even then you were no more developed spiritually than you are today, for reincarnation is progressive, not regressive—that is, you haven't fallen behind where you were in that wise lifetime, and now you can move forward even more.

You may wonder why you should visit only three of your former selves instead of them all. Well, you don't need to. You see, by working in the Timeless Now, it's enough to visit only these three and help them return back home to your celestial parents. When you do so, you'll be set free of their karma, and the effect will domino backward, clearing *all* your former lifetimes.

Remember that in the Timeless Now, you have multiple simultaneous lifetimes that aren't sequential—that is, who you were 2,000 years ago, and the bardo or purgatory you entered into after that death, is still being experienced by these former selves and subtly informing your life today. For the Laika and the physicist, time runs in a linear and nonlinear (or concurrent) fashion. We can also think of these former selves as memories or even genes (which is the way our ancestors "live" within us) that continue to inform us.

When Lisa came to see me, for example, she was cancer-ridden with a catheter dripping chemotherapy into her chest (see p. 88). You'll recall that in her Chamber of Wounds, Lisa discovered a statue with a knife stuck in its heart, after which she spent many months working with her healed soul part and her new soul contracts. Later, we journeyed together to the Upper World to track an alternate destiny to the one she was currently living. There, we found her original self, which had never been touched by illness or disease. Lisa was then shown her entire time line, and she understood how she'd kept injuring her heart time and time again.

Lisa's original self began to inform her destiny, and she was able to heal both her symptoms and her genetic predisposition to cancer. A big piece in her healing was that she was able to let go of fear—after all, her original self always knew that there's no such thing as death. She grew an entirely new cancer-free body, and today she's in better health than ever. She's become an activist dedicated to preserving the environment and a painter—both of which were destinies inscribed in her original soul contract with Spirit.

It's now time to journey to the Upper World. When you meet your celestial parents, you're going to ask them to guide you up the ladder that reaches from the fourth to fifth tier of the Upper World. This level is your ultimate destination, the world of your becoming: your ninth chakra, or Spirit.

Exercise: Journey to the Fifth Plane

Prepare for this journey by opening sacred space. Perform the little-death exercise, and then silently state your intention for this journey—to heal your former selves and discover your original nature. Be open to the possibilities of your destiny, whatever they might be. Follow the journey to the Upper World as you did in the previous chapter, by sending your luminous body into the trunk of a great tree, and coming to a place above the clouds in the thinnest and highest levels of the atmosphere.

You're on a solid cloud where you can stand and walk safely. Now call on the gatekeeper, the Lord of Time, and ask to be allowed to enter his domains. Look into his eyes and state your intent: that you are here to find your original self. Call your celestial parents and ask them to help you find who you were before you were born, before you entered the stream of time. They will take you to the ladder that leads up to the fifth world, where you'll be met by your original self.

Bask for a few minutes in the presence of your original self. Have a hearty laugh at the secret you keep even from yourself and that you will purposefully forget as you leave here: that you are God masquerading as yourself.

Ask your original self to take you to a clear, shallow pool. Look at the pure white sand on the bottom and ask your original self to blow across the surface of the water and call forth the lifetime in which you suffered the most. Watch how the ripples begin to form and reveal the landscape of this lifetime.

Are you a boy or a girl? What color is your skin? Look at your feet—are you walking on grass, sand, or cobblestone? Where is your home? Who are your parents? How did you play? Where is your village or town? Who are your loved ones? How did you grow up? Why did you suffer? Who was your spouse? Did you have children, and if so, who were they? Whom did you lose that you loved? Whom did you hurt? Did you betray someone? Who hurt you? Whom did you not forgive? How were you not forgiven? How did you die?

Ask to fast-forward to the last five minutes of that lifetime to see yourself at your deathbed. See who was with you: Did anybody hold your hand? Who forgave you? Whom did you forgive? And then help that self that was you, but that you no longer are, to die in peace and forgiveness.

Now take a deep breath and tell this self that was you to inhale deeply and exhale, and to set her spirit free. Tell her, "It's okay, my love. It's time to come home, my little one. All is forgiven." See a look of peace and tranquility coming over this self that was once you as she releases her final breath. Follow your soul as it rises from this body and hovers above it for an instant, and then as it goes through the dark tunnel of death to the fourth level of the Upper World. See it being met by your celestial parents and welcomed back home, knowing that all is forgiven.

See the images dissolving back into the sands of time at the bottom of the pool of remembrances, and the water becoming crystal clear once again. Take a deep breath and look into the eyes of your original self and thank her.

Now, ask your original self to breathe again over the pool of remembrances, and to call forth the life in which you had the greatest knowledge and power but abused those gifts because you didn't know how to use them in the right fashion. Watch how the ripples begin to form and reveal the landscape of this life. Are you a boy or a girl? What color is your skin? Look at

your feet—are you walking on grass, sand, or cobblestone? Where is your home? Who are your parents? Where is your village or town? How did you grow up? Whom did you love? How did you love? What were your gifts? Who taught you? What did you learn? How did you misuse your knowledge? How did you abuse your power? Whom did you hurt or betray?

Ask to fast-forward to the last five minutes of that lifetime to see yourself at your deathbed. See who was with you: Did anybody hold your hand? Who forgave you? Whom did you forgive? And then help that self that was you, but that you no longer are, to die in peace and forgiveness.

Tell her, "It's okay, my little one, all is forgiven, it's all right. Come home, my love." See a look of peace and serenity coming over her face. And then help that self take its last breath. Inhale deeply and exhale, release the breath and the spirit with that breath, and follow that spirit as it goes all the way home to your celestial parents.

See the images dissolving back into the sands of time at the bottom of the pool of remembrances, and the water becoming crystal clear once again. Take a deep breath and look into the eyes of your original self and thank her.

Ask to see one final lifetime, in which you had the greatest wisdom and you used it properly to be of service. Begin with your feet—are you wearing sandals or shoes? What color is your skin? How old are you? Are you a boy or a girl? Where do you live? Who are your parents? What did you learn? What were your gifts? Who taught you? How did you use your knowledge? How did you serve? How did you love? How did you live? What difference did you make in the world? Now fast-forward to the last five minutes of that lifetime.

Help this self take its last breath: Inhale deeply and exhale, release the breath and the spirit with that breath, and follow your soul as it returns back home to your celestial parents. Follow your soul as it rises from this body and hovers above it for an instant and goes through the dark tunnel of death to the fourth level of the Upper World. See it being met by your celestial parents and welcomed back home.

See the images dissolving back into the sands of time at the bottom of the pool of remembrances, and the water becoming crystal clear once again. Take a deep breath and look into the eyes of your original self, and thank her.

After you've helped these three former lifetimes to find peace and forgiveness, thank your original self once more. Make a vow to always know who you are, even as you descend back to the fourth tier and your conscious mind forgets, so that God may know Itself through you.

Now turn to your celestial parents and follow them back down the ladder to the fourth tier of the Upper World. If you like, take a moment to visit the village of your ancestors again, and know that all is well with them, that they are at peace. When you've finished, thank your celestial parents.

As you prepare to leave this world, thank the gatekeeper. Go through the clouds and into the uppermost branches of the great tree, descending down the branches, back into the room and into your body, while calling on your winged power animal to accompany you.

Come back to your world, bringing with you knowledge of how you can put your original self to service on Earth. Close sacred space.

As you perform this exercise, visiting the fifth tier regularly, it will reinform every cell in your body, transforming your DNA and allowing you to grow a body that is ageless, that remains supple and flexible, and that doesn't need illness and suffering to learn its lessons in this world. Practice this journey to visit your original self on a daily basis as part of your meditation, and carry this intent to remember your true nature in your heart with purity and compassion.

Dreaming the World into Being

Our destiny is always available to us. As we recognize and embrace our timeless self, we'll be able to grow new bodies and new destinies, which will serve our entire species. In other words, as we heal, the world will heal; as we change, the world will change. No longer guided by the force of karma, humankind will begin to break free of what keeps us bound to strife and conflict, and we'll finally grow into *Homo luminous.*

Inka, Hopi, and Mayan elders sit in meditation, envisioning the world they want their grandchildren to inherit—one in which the rivers and air are clean, there's food for all, and people live in peace with one another. They journey along our collective time lines to find a more harmonious future. This is not the probable future, because they already know what that will be: a world much like the one we're now experiencing—filled with pollution, devastation, and war. Instead, they track for a possible future, no matter how improbable, where people live in harmony with nature, and peace with each other. The sages of old called this "dreaming the world into being."

This is our ultimate task today: to look through a narrow window into the future to find what our species is becoming 10,000 years from now, and to bring that vision back into the present to inform the person we're becoming today. In this way, we can consciously participate in our own evolution to grow bodies that age, heal, and die differently.

We can break free of the grip of fate, which tells us that we're the result of events that happened to us when we were 12 years old (or even from 12 *lifetimes* ago), or that genes we inherited from our parents are waiting to express themselves in a serious malady. When we track our destinies, we can be who we're becoming, not who we've been.

This is your task today. Remember: *You* are the one you've been waiting for.

◎

Afterword

The Altiplano, the vast tundra that goes from Cusco to Lake Titicaca, the sea on top of the world. To the west it drops precipitously into the Amazon, the moist jungle where life continues to evolve and mutate. There, nature is a conjugation of the verb to eat. It is where life depends on eating other life, and life and death are intertwined and inseparable.

But there is another way: our spiritual path, where life is a conjugation of the verb to grow. I remember my Inka mentor telling me that we are here not only to grow corn, but to grow gods. We are gods in becoming. We begin as light from the sun, and now our species is able to dream, splice genes, and take part in the alchemy of life directly. We have a brain that allows us to do this, to experience awareness itself. Now we must flex the muscle of consciousness to dream our world into being, to envision who we're becoming and track the collective destiny of our species.

I bend down to tighten the laces in my boots. The ground is rocky and hard, frozen a few inches below the ground. At 14,000 feet, the sun only warms the uppermost layer of the earth. My boot is resting next to a dandelion—the yellow blossom is close to the ground; it has adapted to the altitude by dispensing with its stem so that the wind will not damage it.

The god-brain . . . I am convinced that meditation is the method the sages of the East employed to access the power of this brain. To us in the West, it serves only as a means of relaxation. To the Laika, meditation is journeying—it is the first step toward accessing the divine within nature and within ourselves. In the Timeless Now, destiny hangs like a ripe fruit for our picking. This is the fruit of the second tree of Eden, the fruit of life everlasting.

I am walking back to Eden. The energy that pours into the earth from the sun courses through me like the blood that flows through my veins. I raise my gaze to the distant mountains, to my destination, to the headwaters of the Amazon, to the spring of its birth.

— from Alberto's journal[1]

Acknowledgments

There are many persons who contributed to the creation of this book. First and foremost I'd like to thank Susan Emerling and Greg Zelonka, without whom this book would never have been born. And my editors Nancy Peske, Jill Kramer, Shannon Littrell, and Chris Morris shaped and sculpted the manuscript into life.

I'd also like to thank Reid Tracy, president of Hay House, for his vision of what this book could become; my assistants Rhonda Bryant and Ranni Weiss for diligently typing and retyping the manuscript; and my friends Sally Nelson, Naomi Silverstone, Amanda Anderson, Susan Reiner, Lynn Berryhill, and Helen Fost for reviewing and commenting on the book as it took shape. I'm grateful to Ellen Ostroth for the weeks she spent collecting soul-retrieval cases from our students, and to Marcela Villalobos for her care and loving encouragement.

Last, I'd like to thank Linda Fitch for holding the vision of The Four Winds Society and helping me teach our students to master the practices of soul retrieval and destiny retrieval.

Alberto Villoldo
www.thefourwinds.com

Endnotes

Chapter Five

1. All journal entries with footnotes have been reprinted from the following: Villoldo, Alberto, and Erik Jendresen. *The Four Winds: A Shaman's Odyssey into the Amazon.* New York: HarperCollins, 1992. The entries without footnotes have come from the author's personal writings.

Chapter Six

1. Ibid.

Chapter Eight

1. Ibid.
2. Andrews, Ted. *Animal-Speak: The Spiritual & Magical Powers of Creatures Great & Small.* St. Paul, Minnesota: Llewellyn Publications, 1993.

Chapter Nine

1. Frankl, Viktor E. *Man's Search for Meaning.* New York: Simon & Schuster, 1963.

Chapter Eleven

1. For a description of the Tibetan journey beyond death, see *The Tibetan Book of Living and Dying* by Sogyal Rinpoche.
2. Moody, Raymond. *Reflections on Life After Life.* New York: Bantam, 1985.

Chapter Twelve

1. Villoldo and Jendresen. *The Four Winds.*
2. Genetic theory and Darwin's theory of natural selection tell us that evolution happens in between generations and that natural selection, the gradual weeding out of the less-fit members of the species, will slowly guide the course of evolution.
3. I would like to thank Bill Smith for this insight.

Afterword

1. Villoldo and Jendresen. *The Four Winds.*

About the Author

Alberto Villoldo, Ph.D., a psychologist and medical anthropologist, has studied the healing practices of the Amazon and Inka shamans for more than 25 years. While at San Francisco State University, he founded the Biological Self-Regulation Laboratory to study how the mind creates psychosomatic health and disease.

Villoldo directs The Four Winds Society, where he trains individuals throughout the world in the practice of energy medicine and soul retrieval. He has training centers in New England; California; the U.K.; Holland; and Park City, Utah.

The author of the bestseller *Shaman, Healer, Sage,* Villoldo now draws on his vast knowledge to bring us a practical and revolutionary way to discover the source of an original wound that may have occurred during childhood or in a former lifetime, and that derailed our destiny. He then shows us how to track forward along our time lines to find our best and highest future.

An avid skier, hiker, and mountaineer, he leads annual expeditions to the Amazon and the Andes to work with the wisdom teachers of the Americas.

Website: **www.thefourwinds.com**

Hay House Titles of Related Interest

The Alchemist's Handbook, by John Randolph Price

American Indian Prophecies: Conversations with Chasing Deer, by Kurt Kaltreider, Ph.D.

Archangels & Ascended Masters: A Guide to Working and Healing with Divinities and Deities, by Doreen Virtue, Ph.D.

The God Code: The Secret of Our Past, the Promise of Our Future, by Gregg Braden

The Love and Power Journal: A Workbook for the Art of Living, by Lynn V. Andrews

Mirrors of Time: Using Regression for Physical, Emotional, and Spiritual Healing, by Brian L. Weiss, M.D.

Mother God: The Feminine Principle to Our Creator, by Sylvia Browne

Power Animals: How to Connect with Your Animal Spirit Guide, by Steven D. Farmer, Ph.D.

7 Paths to God: *The Ways of the Mystic,* by Joan Borysenko, Ph.D.

Sixth Sense: *Including the Secrets of the Etheric Subtle Body,*
by Stuart Wilde

Soul Coaching: *28 Days to Discover Your Authentic Self,* by Denise Linn

Spirit Medicine: *Healing in the Sacred Realms,*
by Hank Wesselman, Ph.D., and Jill Kuykendall, RPT

Visionseeker: *Shared Wisdom from the Place of Refuge,*
by Hank Wesselman, Ph.D.

All of the above are available at
your local bookstore, or may be ordered by visiting:

Hay House USA: **www.hayhouse.com**
Hay House Australia: **www.hayhouse.com.au**
Hay House UK: **www.hayhouse.co.uk**
Hay House South Africa: **www.hayhouse.co.za**
Hay House India: **www.hayhouse.co.in**

Notes

Notes

Notes

Notes

Notes

Notes

Notes

Notes

We hope you enjoyed this Hay House book.
If you'd like to receive our online catalog featuring additional
information on Hay House books and products, or if you'd
like to find out more about the Hay Foundation, please contact:

Hay House, Inc.
P.O. Box 5100
Carlsbad, CA 92018-5100

(760) 431-7695 or **(800) 654-5126**
(760) 431-6948 (fax) or **(800) 650-5115** (fax)
www.hayhouse.com®

Published and distributed in Australia by: Hay House Australia Pty. Ltd.,
18/36 Ralph St., Alexandria NSW 2015 • *Phone:* 612-9669-4299
Fax: 612-9669-4144 • www.hayhouse.com.au

Published and distributed in the United Kingdom by: Hay House UK, Ltd.,
292B Kensal Rd., London W10 5BE • *Phone:* 44-20-8962-1230
Fax: 44-20-8962-1239 • www.hayhouse.co.uk

Published and distributed in the Republic of South Africa by:
Hay House SA (Pty), Ltd., P.O. Box 990, Witkoppen 2068
Phone/Fax: 27-11-467-8904 • www.hayhouse.co.za

Published in India by: Hay House Publishers India, Muskaan Complex, Plot
No. 3, B-2, Vasant Kunj, New Delhi 110 070 • *Phone:* 91-11-4176-1620
Fax: 91-11-4176-1630 • www.hayhouse.co.in

Distributed in Canada by: Raincoast, 9050 Shaughnessy St., Vancouver,
B.C. V6P 6E5 • *Phone:* (604) 323-7100 • *Fax:* (604) 323-2600
www.raincoast.com

Take Your Soul on a Vacation

Visit **www.HealYourLife.com**® to regroup, recharge,
and reconnect with your own magnificence.
Featuring blogs, mind-body-spirit news, and life-changing
wisdom from Louise Hay and friends.

Visit **www.HealYourLife.com** today!